GONCHAROV

BY

JANKO LAVRIN

NEW YORK / RUSSELL & RUSSELL

First published in 1954 in the Series
Studies in Modern European Literature and Thought
by Bowes & Bowes Publishers Limited, Cambridge

REISSUED, 1969, BY RUSSELL & RUSSELL
A DIVISION OF ATHENEUM PUBLISHERS, INC.
BY ARRANGEMENT WITH BOWES & BOWES PUBLISHERS LIMITED, LONDON
L. C. CATALOG CARD NO: 68-27070
PRINTED IN THE UNITED STATES OF AMERICA

Quotations from *A Common Story* are taken from Constance Garnett's translation, published by Messrs Heinemann in 1890 and 1917. Those from *Oblomov* are taken from Natalie Duddington's version, published by Messrs Allen and Unwin in 1929, and by Messrs Dent (London) and Dutton (New York) in 'Everyman's Library' in 1932. The author expresses his thanks to the publishers concerned. All other quotations have been translated by the author.

J. L.

CONTENTS

I.   A Biographical Survey   9

II. A Common Story   18

III. Oblomov and Oblomovism   27

IV. The Ravine   37

V.   Expedition, Reminiscences and Polemics   47

VI. Goncharov's Realism   53

VII. Conclusion   60

Biographical Note   61

Bibliography   62

I

A Biographical Survey

Although one of the foremost novelists in Russia and author of the world classic *Oblomov*, Ivan Alexandrovich Goncharov is still little known outside his own country. This may be due partly to the fact that he was devoid of any of those vagaries of genius which were conspicuous in some other great figures of Russian letters: in Tolstoy, for instance, in Gogol, or in Dostoevsky. As a private individual Goncharov was in fact the very picture of what might be called respectable conformity. It is true that in later life he became a prey to certain mental and nervous troubles, but these were of a purely clinical type—neither colourful nor exceptional enough to draw much attention. Otherwise he was almost too 'prosaic' and too methodical for the popular conception of a great artist. Intent on becoming a success both as writer and civil servant, he marched towards this double goal in a deliberate, even somewhat calculated manner. In literature, at any rate, he succeeded well enough, for he was ushered into fame by his very first novel (in 1847) almost as a matter of course. Some twelve years later his national reputation hardly lagged behind that of Turgenev, Dostoevsky and Tolstoy, and has remained high ever since; so much so that it is now impossible to talk of the leading Russian realists without mentioning Goncharov. But this only makes it the more imperative for us to know at least the important facts about him and his work.

Born in June, 1812, in the remote Volga town of Simbirsk (now Ulyanovsk), Goncharov came of a well-to-do merchant family with gentry traditions. His parents lived in the approved 'noble' manner, with plenty of house-serfs and all sorts of other insignia required by that style and status. Their house was situated in the town, but its character was more like that of a country mansion on the banks of the Volga, with magnificent vistas opening up from its grounds. As Ivan had lost his father at the age of seven, his mother Avdotya Matveyevna, a homely and practical woman, brought up her four children (two boys and two girls) according to the old-fashioned patriarchal notions which lingered on in the provinces with a tenacity of their own. She, moreover, became the manageress

9

of the not too distant estate belonging to a certain N.N. Tregubov, an ex-naval officer who had settled down in Simbirsk
as a tenant of Mme Goncharova and almost as a member of her
family. Ivan—his favourite—was thus exposed from an early
age to a double set of impressions and, therefore, to a double
set of values. One of them was conditioned by the pleasantly
indolent manor-tradition with its atmosphere of the past, while
the other came from the enterprizing mercantile bourgeoisie at
a time when the old patriarchal system of Russia—a system
based on serfdom—was already showing the cracks and portents
of its forthcoming doom.

This double strain was characteristic of Goncharov throughout
the whole of his life. He loved the stabilized forms of existence
which hailed from the past—loved them with a hidden romantic attachment. At the same time there was in him the sober
bourgeois who saw clearly the need of a more modern, more
active type of life, and who looked with scepticism at his own
romantic leanings. His head, if not his heart, was on the side
of the various up-to-date factors which he accepted as a mark of
progress. But while evaluating progress above all in terms of
activities such as were known in the West, he yet remained
rooted in the pleasantly somnolent existence typical of the old
patriarchal Russian families, especially of those living in such
remote corners as Simbirsk.

The conflict between these two trends (the eternal conflict
between the old and the new) found an original expression in
Goncharov and in his work. He saw in it a vital dilemma,
which he actually turned into the *Leitmotif* of his novels. This
he did against the background of Russia's belated transition
from a feudal or semi-feudal economic system to a more modern
bourgeois-capitalist pattern of existence. Goncharov's novels
can claim to be an epic of this transition, or—if you prefer—of
this struggle. For it was a struggle which, in a way, was taking
place also in the author's own consciousness. Divided between
his allegiance to the past and his sympathies with the dawning
new era, he embodied in his writings certain features of this
process with a skill which takes his literary work beyond a
mere local or a mere temporary significance. But in order to
understand the deeper aspects of Goncharov the writer we
must first mention something about Goncharov the man. In
this case, at any rate, knowing one helps us to appreciate the
other.

When talking of Goncharov's early impressionable years, one should bear in mind that they were spent in circumstances which prevented him from witnessing the social and moral abuses of serfdom. At home, as well as during his occasional visits to the Tregubov's estate, he saw only the pleasant and 'idyllic' side of it. Nor was there any lack of warmth or affection among the members of the Goncharov family. Tregubov, on the other hand, brought a note of romance with his tales about the sea which were always a treat for the children. In this atmosphere the boy developed a passion for reading even before he was sent —at the age of nine—to the parson Troitsky whose German wife ran a small but select boarding school on the opposite bank of the Volga. Here he was taught French and German, to which he later added a smattering of English. In 1822 he went, together with his elder brother Nikolai, to Moscow, where he pined for several years in an atrocious School of Commerce, until in 1831 he entered the University. During his University years his taste for literature was fostered above all by the spell of Pushkin's works and by the lectures of Professor N. Nadezhdin—a violent opponent of Russian (or any other) romanticism.

The interests prevalent among the students of Moscow University during the early 1830's were however largely romantic and affected by German idealistic philosophy. Those were the years when the famous Stankevich circle—with such members as the young Belinsky, K. Aksakov, Bakunin, Katkov, Granovsky—brought a new spirit to the rising generation. Parallel with that group, Alexander Herzen gathered around him students who were more concerned with the social and political problems of the time. But Goncharov seemed to be little drawn towards activities of this kind, and took no part in them.

After his graduation he returned, in the summer of 1834, to his native Simbirsk. At home he was welcomed not only by his family but also by the local 'society', or rather by that mixture of officials and provincial landowners which passed for such. He even took a post in the civil service, but he soon found Simbirsk something of a dead end. So he left it and went to Petersburg where he became a translator in the Ministry of Finance and worked for fifteen years without any visible advance in his career. It is doubtful whether he ever relished his official duties, but on the surface he adapted himself well enough to the obligatory bureaucratic routine. Many years after, when looking back at it all, he complained in a letter (1865) that in spite of a continuous urge to write he had been all the time compelled to slave as an official under the leaden sky of Petersburg, without being able to spare even a whole month each year for the work he really wanted to do. There were of course compensations. He found them above all in the family of the artist N. A. Maikov, to whose two sons[1] he taught Russian literature.

As Maikov's house was a kind of literary salon, its atmosphere must have been stimulating. Goncharov, however, was in no hurry to assert himself as a writer. As if diffident of his own talent he was reluctant to take the plunge. The only literary products he disclosed during those early years at Petersburg were four not very promising poems he gave to Maikov for the private miscellany *Podsnezhnik* (*The Snowdrop*) in 1835-36.[2] A humorous story, *Likhaya bolest* (*A Bad Ailment*) appeared in the same miscellany in 1838. A year later he made a further contribution with the story, *Schastlivaya oshibka* (*A Lucky Error*) in another private miscellany, *Lunnye nochi* (*The Moon Nights*). It is a fashionable 'high-life' story about the love of a young man-about-town for a rather spoilt and capricious Petersburg beauty. After a final quarrel with her he is invited to a ball at the Merchants Assembly, but owing to his coachman's error he is taken to a ball at the Neapolitan Embassy instead. Here he suddenly finds the lady of his heart in a contrite and unhappy mood. A reconciliation follows, with the prospect of a wedding and other blessings at the end of it all. Devoid of any excessive merit, the story can yet claim attention as a promise of bigger things to come.

While continuing to train his talent, Goncharov came to the conclusion that his real genre was not the short story but the novel, which he obviously regarded as the chief literary vehicle for all the complexities of modern life. So he embarked upon a novel of his own and worked at it with his methodical perseverance. When it was practically finished he met in 1846 the 'furious' Vissarion Belinsky whose critical essays were destined to leave such a profound mark on Russian literature. A greater contrast than that between Goncharov (now a correct, cold and somewhat dandified civil servant) and the temperamental Belinsky

---

[1] Apollon, subsequently a poet, and Valerian who became one of the most promising literary critics, but died very young.

[2] Goncharov's actual literary début was made in 1832, when Nadezhdin's periodical, *Telescope*, printed his translation of two chapters from *Atar-Gull* by Eugène Sue.

could hardly be imagined. Nevertheless the two men seem to have got on quite well even if, gradually, their relations became more reserved—which was to be expected. Anyway, it was Belinsky who in 1847 greeted Goncharov's *Obyknovennaya istoriya* (*A Common Story*) with enthusiasm and thus established its reputation at once. In 1848 Goncharov's humorous Petersburg sketch *Ivan Savich Podzhabrin* (written some six years earlier) appeared and was soon followed by his excellent *Son Oblomova* (*Oblomov's Dream*, 1849) which he later incorporated in his novel *Oblomov*.

During the twelve years that elapsed between *A Common Story* and *Oblomov*, Goncharov took part in a long and adventurous sea journey to the Far East—as secretary to the Russian expedition whose task it was to open commercial relations with Japan. The expedition, led by Admiral Putyatin, lasted some two years (1852-54) and was later described by Goncharov in a number of travel sketches. These were collected and published in his voluminous *Fregat Pallada* (*The Frigate Pallas*) in 1858. A couple of years before its publication he had been transferred to the department of censorship where he may have been able to mitigate at least some of the evils of that unsavoury institution. Meanwhile, his novel *Oblomov*, published in 1859, moved its author into the front rank of the Russian realists. Especially after N. A. Dobrolyubov's enlightening essay in *Sovremennik* (*The Contemporary*, May 1859) this new product of Goncharov's pen was proclaimed a masterpiece even if judged by the severest standards.

Finding the duties of a censor both monotonous and irksome,[1] Goncharov retired at the beginning of 1860, but two years later he was appointed editor of the official newspaper, *Severnaya pochta* (*The Northern Mail*). In another ten months or so he was relieved of this post only to become a member of the almighty Press Council, doing censorship once more—this time on a higher rung of the bureaucratic ladder. The very routine of his new duties now required a more conservative complexion than Goncharov (always a liberal at heart) had cared to display hitherto. But having got used to political mimicry, he acquitted himself tactfully enough. As a result in 1867 he was able to retire with a pension and the rank of a State Councillor. The years that followed were the uneventful years of an ageing bachelor

[1] Goncharov the censor was violently attacked, on December 1st, 1857, in the famous Russian periodical *Kólokol* (*The Bell*), edited and published by Alexander Herzen in London.

who, on account of bad health, had often to stay abroad, mainly in Austria and Germany.

Soon after his retirement he published his third and last novel, *Obryv* (*The Ravine*) which appeared in 1869, ten years after *Oblomov*. Here for the first time Goncharov the artist had something of an 'ideological' axe to grind. The novel, naturally, caused much controversy and irritation. Tired and as if bored by it all, he no longer contemplated writing another major work. 'I feel so incredibly bored wherever I go', he wrote at the time to his sister Anna. Nor was he anxious to cultivate extensive literary contacts. One of the few authors he had befriended was the poet and dramatist Count Alexey K. Tolstoy whose talent he rated very high. He continued to print, from time to time, things of a miscellaneous character, but on the whole he wrote little. Hampered by illness, by boredom, and by a growing diffidence towards human beings, he began to show signs of an unbalanced mind, the causes of which may have been due to heredity: his father, his elder brother Nikolai and one of his two sisters seemed to have suffered from occasional mental troubles. Goncharov's case became, moreover, complicated by his old and rather strange professional jealousy of another great writer—Ivan Turgenev.

3

The tense relations and rows between Tolstoy and Turgenev are well known. So are the misunderstandings between Turgenev and Dostoevsky. We are less acquainted, though, with the quarrels between Goncharov and Turgenev, quarrels which are of considerable psychological as well as literary interest. The initiative in this respect came from Goncharov whose outbursts against his *confrère* were due to secret envy and to quite a few rankling 'complexes' besides. The very fact that Goncharov had hesitated to publish his first novel until he was thirty-five proves that, whatever his ambitions, he was not over-sure of his talent. Self-conscious and diffident by nature, he did not care to mix too much with acknowledged authors either—as though afraid of awakening thereby the feeling of his own inferiority. If we are to believe Panayev's *Memoirs*[1], Goncharov met Gogol

[1] Panayev, a minor author of the Belinsky circle, bought, in 1846, together with the poet Nekrasov, the periodical *Sovremennik* (*The Contemporary*) which had been founded by Pushkin in 1836, but after his death began to deteriorate. Under Nekrasov and Panayev it soon became the foremost radical periodical in Russia.

only once, in 1848, and even that very brief encounter was evidently far from happy. His prolonged stay in a minor rank of the civil service was itself enough to foster his caution, shyness, and fear of anything that might put him into a ridiculous position. As a writer, again, he worked very slowly and painstakingly, which was a further reason for doubt and despondency. His literary success was welcomed by him as a definite proof of his talent. Yet while appreciative of his new status on the ladder of fame, he was prone to resent any competition that might have jeopardized it.

The only serious rival at the beginning of his career was Ivan Turgenev. True enough, Turgenev's serialized *Zapiski okhotnika* (*A Sportman's Sketches*), which started in 1847, was eclipsed by Goncharov's first novel, but not for long. Each subsequent work published by Turgenev was a literary triumph. Still, the relations between the two authors were quite tolerable until, in 1859, a first serious breach occurred. This was the year when Turgenev's *Dvoryanskoe gnezdo* (*A Nest of Gentlefolk*) appeared almost simultaneously with Goncharov's *Oblomov*. Turgenev's novel took the public by storm, whereas *Oblomov*, with its slow pace, was only gradually sized up at its true value. Goncharov felt hurt. Remembering that he had often discussed with Turgenev plots and situations he wanted to make use of in his next novel, *The Ravine*, he now suddenly became convinced that his literary rival, having taken advantage of his trust, was plagiarizing him. Goncharov's tactless letters only made matters worse, although Turgenev behaved throughout the affair with patience and composure. When at the beginning of 1860 Turgenev's novel *Nakanune* (*On the Eve*) came out, Goncharov sent him—on March 3rd—another clumsy letter in which he repeated the same allegations.[1] Owing to Turgenev's demand, an arbitration conducted by other fellow-writers was arranged on March 29th. Turgenev was exonerated, but as he did not like the wording of the judgment the breach between the two authors continued until 1864, when it was temporarily patched up.

In the winter of 1867-68 their relations were broken once again and for good. This time Goncharov's behaviour began to assume a decidedly alarming and even pathological nature. The curious

[1] There are certain superficial resemblances between Raisky, the hero of *The Ravine*, and Panshin in Turgenev's *The Nest of Gentlefolk*; also between Vera in *The Ravine* and Helena in Turgenev's *On the Eve*.

point in the whole affair was that Goncharov might have remained at peace if Turgenev had continued to write short stories instead of novels. In his eyes it was Turgenev the novelist who threatened to steal the laurels of the novelist Goncharov. And since Turgenev was incorrigible in this respect, his accuser had no choice but to nurse his suspicion and rage. Once, while taking a walk in the Summer Park at Petersburg, the two authors were in danger of suddenly meeting each other. Goncharov spotted his rival from afar and immediately began to run away, shouting at the top of his voice: 'A thief! A thief!'

His state of health was of course an extenuating circumstance. But this only made things all the worse for him. In some of his letters to Alexey K. Tolstoy, Goncharov showed unmistakable signs of persecution mania. He often imagined himself to be surrounded by spies and plotters led by that arch-plotter of evil, Ivan Turgenev. 'Yesterday there was a cold wind, clouds came —my soul was oppressed by it all and once more dregs emerged from it', he wrote in 1868 to the editor and literary historian M. M. Stasyulevich, only one year after his final retirement. 'I threw away my pen, bent my head—and began to see, in a waking state, the nasty dreams which keep on persecuting me! Again friendly faces began to turn into enemies, wink at me from the corners, bespatter me with mud, put me to the pillar of shame, without being able to grasp or understand anything of my many-sided nature, of my imagination, or of my writings. I began to suffocate, I wanted to jump into the water, into the fire, into a world different from the one we live in, to depart altogether from this world.'

It must have been in one of such moods that Goncharov concocted that curious piece of invective, *Neobyknovennaya istoriya* (*The Uncommon Story*), referring to his feud with his old rival, Turgenev. Written in the second half of the 1870's, this manuscript came to light only recently, and was first printed in 1924. It is a kind of personal confession containing a malicious portrait of Turgenev, who is here charged with literary robbery. According to Goncharov, Turgenev had plagiarized, and repeatedly so, *The Ravine*, while that novel was still in the process of being written. He moreover (so Goncharov thought) must have transmitted a number of stolen passages to Flaubert, who made use of them in *L'éducation sentimentale*, and even to the German author Berthold Auerbach for *Das Landhaus am Rhein*. Suffering from this obsession, Goncharov now kept all his

16

manuscripts under lock and key, lest Turgenev should viciously break in again and steal some further ideas and materials.

Once in the grip of such suspicions, Goncharov drifted towards the isolated existence of a recluse. In the end he became diffident of everybody except his German valet Treigult. He was averse even to seeing his own works reprinted; and as for his correspondence, he eventually burned most of the letters that had been written to him. The *auto-da-fé* may have included some of his manuscripts as well. At the same time he implored his friends—in print—never to publish the letters he had written to them, with the result that some of these, too, were destroyed. His persecution mania thus seems to have made him frightened of contact with the outside world even through correspondence. In 1878 Treigult's widow became his housekeeper. It was to her and her three children (of whom he was inordinately fond) that he bequeathed his estate. Filled with apathy and half-blind, he had a stroke in 1888, after which, in his Petersburg flat, he waited with resignation for the end. It came in September, 1891.

4

Whatever Goncharov's personal faults and virtues, his three novels, and especially *Oblomov*, would entitle him to a place of honour in any literature. His is one of the big names in Russian and in European realism as a whole. And since the word 'realism' has been mentioned, we might as well refer to the fact that for a long time Goncharov was regarded as one of the most detached and objective painters of life. Belinsky insisted on it, and so did Dobrolyubov. More recently, however, objections to this interpretation have arisen. An authority such as Professor E. Lyatsky has been so anxious to prove the essentially subjective character of Goncharov's work that he has gone to the other extreme.

The truth is of course somewhere between these two views. All good observers, however detached, are *also* subjective for the very reason that each has only his own pair of eyes and his own personal way of looking at things. Moreover, it is only through self-observation that we learn how to observe others. No matter how detached we try to be in this process, we cannot help putting into other people's souls and minds first of all that which we find in ourselves. Only a photographic realist (or 'protocolist') who has eyes and no imagination can indulge in

17

that cold observation for its own sake which has nothing to do with creative art as such, and which was foreign to Goncharov. For however 'objective' his chief characters, he projected at least into some of them dilemmas and inhibitions from which he himself suffered. In this respect his process of writing was also a process of catharsis, of liberation. It is quite possible that had he continued on the same scale and in the same direction after *The Ravine*, he might have been spared some of those pathological ordeals which embittered the last years of his life.

The very *Leitmotif*—the eternal struggle between the old and the new—recurring in his novels is significant. It points to something similar in Goncharov's own mind. And the measure of his art is precisely the skill with which he was yet able to detach this conflict in such a way as to turn several of his characters into realistic symbols representing entire social and psychological categories. The language in which he did it may be less idiomatic than that of some other great fellow-writers, yet it always has a lucid conversational flow and a naturalness which is devoid of anything studied, no matter how long and laborious his creative process may have been at times. Lastly, Goncharov belongs not only to the period for which he wrote. Where and how far did he transcend it? Can his work be of real interest if evaluated from the angle of our present-day views and attitudes? After all, the final test of an author, to whatever age he may belong chronologically, is his importance for us. But Goncharov need not fear a test of this kind.

II

A Common Story

I

The year 1847, in which Goncharov's first novel, *Obyknovennaya istoriya* (*A Common Story*), appeared, was a great vintage year in the annals of Russian literature—a true *annus mirabilis* if judged by the quality of writings it produced. These included the poignant narrative from peasant life, *Anton Goremyka* by Dmitry Grigorovich; the psychological novel *Kto vinovat* (*Whose Fault*) by Alexander Herzen; the George-Sandian *Polinka Saks* by V. Druzhinin; and the first of those stories by Turgenev which created something of a furore when, in 1852, they were published in book form as *Zapiski okhotnika* (*A Sportman's Sketches*). Alexey Pisemsky entered literature in the same year with his scathing novel, *Boyarshchina*, which was, however, forbidden by the censor. Also the remarkable realistic playwright Alexander Ostrovsky made his début in 1847.

All this was done in the style and spirit of the 'natural school' championed by Belinsky, who demanded from literature a realistic approach to life as well as 'naturalness', as distinct from the rhetorical artificialities of many a romantic writer. After the 'little man' had been sanctioned in Russian letters, above all by Gogol's *Shinel* (*The Greatcoat*, 1842), Dmitry Grigorovich's narrative *Derevnya* (*The Village*, 1846) made the serf fashionable in Russian fiction, but with a sentimental-philanthropic accent à la George Sand. The same spirit prevails in his *Anton Goremyka* (literally *Anton the Hapless*), published a year later. Following Belinsky's injunctions, the younger authors began to study real people and real problems, while exposing the evils they saw around, beginning with those of serfdom. In this manner literature, having abandoned its escapist trend, served life and yet remained literature in its own right. The aggressive critical realism of Gogol was welcomed by them. In addition there was the impact of the 'classical realist' Pushkin, not to mention Lermontov whose crisp analytical novel,*Geroy nashego, vremeni* (*A Hero of our Time*, 1840), towered as a pioneering work of its kind.

The task was complicated by a number of aspects and dilemmas at a time when Russia had to cope with the gradual replacement of her feudal agricultural system by a pattern based mainly on money. Even the early phases of such a process were bound to dislocate the traditional social-economic pattern of the country, and indeed the very habits of life and thought of that class which hitherto had thrived on the system of serfdom. A new orientation, with all sorts of changes, became imperative for the gentry who owned both the land and the serfs. Under the pressure of encroaching capitalism many an impoverished or bankrupt landowner found himself a social *déclassé*, while the enterprizing 'commoners' (Belinsky was one of them) asserted themselves more and more persistently in the economic and cultural life of the country. An interesting product of the *rapprochement*, or rather of the fusion of these two elements, was the emergence of the 'intelligentsia' which, from the 1840's onwards right up to the revolution of 1917, was destined to play the most prominent part in the inner development of Russia.

Yet the change itself must have been difficult for the members of the gentry-class. Many of them were neither quick nor willing enough to adapt themselves to the new forces which kept undermining their old habits. The 'superfluous man', i.e. the individual who belonged nowhere because he had been put out of gear by economic circumstances and by history itself, became rather typical of those years. Typical also was the frequent though often sterile awareness that, whatever the difficulties, a more up-to-date way of life was imperative and, in fact, imminent.

Such, on the whole, was the position of Goncharov at the time he wrote his first novel. He may have remained a stranger to some of the deeper mental processes of the generation of the 1840's. Still, one of the cardinal dilemmas of that decade—the struggle between the old and the new, between 'fathers' and 'children'—was clear enough to him, and he presented it, with surprising competence, in *A Common Story*, both on the psychological and the social plane. He began writing the novel certainly not later than 1844, but rewrote it several times before he gave it its final shape. In 1846 the manuscript came into the hands of the poet Nekrasov, who showed it to Belinsky. In the following year it appeared in *Sovremennik* (*The Contemporary*) and was proclaimed the best work of fiction since Gogol's *Dead Souls* (1842). In his survey of Russian literature for 1847, Belinsky praised above all Goncharov's lively dialogue and his full-length portraits, especially those of the women. In a letter to his friend V. P. Botkin he moreover defined the novel as a splendid blow to sentimental romanticism and provincialism.[1] This it certainly was, but it was also many things besides. The central problem, i.e. the need for a radical change in the outlook and in the way of life, was simple to the point of baldness. Yet the skill and the neat precision with which Goncharov worked it out were more than creditable, especially in a first novel.

2

Since the structure of *A Common Story* is based on the antithesis between what was and what ought to be, the two principal figures, Alexander Aduyev[2] and his uncle Peter Aduyev, are

[1] It may be of interest that in *A Common Story* the author parodied his own romantic lyrics written in 1835 and 1836 for *The Snowdrop*.
[2] This name was used by Goncharov in his early story, *A Lucky Error*.

contrasted accordingly. So are their respective backgrounds: the peaceful and idyllic country-estate Grachi on the one hand, and the bustling life in Petersburg on the other. The novel opens with the preparations for Alexander's departure for Petersburg, where his uncle, an enterprising man of about forty, holds a high post in the bureaucratic world as well as in the world of business, with all sorts of honours as the obvious outcome of such activities. His young nephew, who is about to join him, is however made of different material. In spite of his University education, he is a provincial romantic whose roots and notions of life are inseparable from the pleasant if soporific atmosphere of his ancestral estate.

From the balcony came a fresh scent. Around the house far into the distance stretched the garden, full of lime trees, thick wild roses, berries, and bushes of lilac. And among the trees were beds of bright-coloured flowers, and here and there, little paths ran zigzagging in and out, while in the distance was a softly splashing lake, on one side golden with rays of the morning sun and smooth as glass, on the other as dark-blue as the sky mirrored in it, and stirred by faint ripples. And then an amphitheatre formed by the fields of waving corn and bordered by a dark forest.

Such was the homely paradise in the midst of which Alexander's childhood and youth had passed. His education, too, had been in perfect agreement with it.

From his nursery onwards life had been all smiles for him —his mother idolized him and spoilt him, as mothers do spoil an only son; his nurses sang to him in his cradle that he would walk in gold and never know sorrow; his teachers declared that he would do something great, and, in addition to the adoration of his household, the daughter of their neighbour smiled on him. And the old cat, Vaska, seemed to be more amiable to him than to anyone else in the house. Sorrow, tears, trouble—all that he knew only by hearsay ... so the future presented itself to him in rainbow colours. Something beckoned to him in the distance, but precisely what he could not tell. Seductive phantoms glimmered before him, but he could never catch a close view of them; he could hear mingled sounds—now the voice of glory, now the voice of love—and all moved him to a sweet unrest.

21

Infected by this 'sweet unrest', and probably also by the vague echoes of the *Zeitgeist*, this day-dreamer decided to try the emporium of all great ambitions—Petersburg. One of his dreams was to become a famous poet and writer under the wing of that sentimental romanticism which in the provinces had often assumed a peculiarly naïve and jejune character, so well depicted by Pushkin in the poet Lensky (*Evgeny Onegin*). But once in the Russian capital, Alexander was confronted by his worldly-wise and rather caustic uncle Peter Aduyev, who belonged to the new up-to-date species of man. A realist to the marrow of his bones, he combined an active though cold efficiency with a philistine love of wealth and comfort. He also prided himself on that 'progressive' outlook which made him grasp the needs of the epoch and stride forward without ever doubting either his abilities or his judgment.

The meeting between this man and Alexander was remarkable on account of the contrast between the two. It was only with reluctance that the uncle grudgingly consented to help him. As though chuckling at his nephew's provincial exuberance, he procured him a modest official post plus the commission to translate for a periodical articles on manure, potato starch and suchlike subjects. It was not much of a career, but it made Alexander shed at least some of his rustic habits. In two years' time he began to resemble a man-about-town who was able to control his emotions and even his highfalutin' language. Yet at bottom he remained the same naïve fellow as before and continued to cherish his exalted dreams, of love in particular. So, step by step, he had to undergo a cruel *éducation sentimentale* which made him lose one illusion after the other, beginning with the 'sacred mystery' of love. His uncle (anxious to undermine his dreams) gave him a timely warning that 'your love will be just like other people's, neither deeper nor stronger; the only difference is that you will believe in eternal, unchanging love, and will think about nothing else, and that is just what is so silly; you are preparing for yourself more unhappiness than you need'. And he was right.

Alexander's first love was Nadinka—a capricious and elusive minx, not unlike the heroine of *A Lucky Error*. Full of ardent vows, she yet jilted him as soon as a more desirable suitor presented himself. This was Alexander's first, but by no means his last, *illusion perdue*. In due course he became infatuated with Julia, who loved according to the tempestuous romances she had read, and 'abandoned herself to her passion as a rider at

22

a gallop abandons himself to his horse'. Their love was an affair of mutual 'sincere outpourings of the heart' in the approved romantic style. But the more devoted she became the colder he grew, without knowing why. There was no obstacle to their happiness; yet before long he started yawning in her presence, and eventually gave her up in a most callously unromantic manner.

A fleeting and not very creditable love affair with another girl followed, but its usual consummation was frustrated in the nick of time by the girl's father. Sick of it all, disappointed with love, with his literary ambitions, with his civil service, Alexander could think of nothing better than blaming his uncle, whose rôle of mentor had borne such meagre fruits. 'You started a conflict in me between two opposing views of life and I could not reconcile them; what has còme of it? Everything in me has been reduced to a state of doubt, a kind of chaos.' On the advice of his uncle (now suitably married), Alexander resigned himself to failure. A 'disgrace to the name of Aduyev', he went back to his distant estate, hoping to find there a haven of peace. Seven years of disappointments in the capital had reduced him, to the consternation of his mother, almost to the shadow of his former self. Still, he was now at home where all the de eperelements of his being were focused and where he felt at one with the people and with the surrounding landscape. A year and a half of the quiet country existence restored his health, yet he began to experience troubles of a different kind. Having once tasted of the hectic life of the capital, he was unable to endure the countryside for long. His idyllic paradise became a well of ennui which made him more and more restless. In the end he decided to flee from it and from himself. So he returned to Petersburg in order to make a new start, this time following in all earnest his uncle's precepts.

In the Epilogue to the novel he is shown to us four years later. But what a change! Bald, stout and rosy, he is now flushed with success and on the eve of marrying an heiress. Ironically enough, he struts about as an improved edition of his uncle at the very moment when the latter has begun to wonder whether there is any sense in all the riches he himself had piled up for their own sake. Under the influence of his sensitive and somewhat unhappy wife, who is quite aware of the emptiness of a bourgeois marriage devoid of inner content, Aduyev senior is plunged into despondency precisely when his dapper nephew is about to outstrip him in the things which in the end cannot but prove to be 'vanity of vanities'.

A Common Story is thus told with a consistent obviousness,
behind which there is a scarcely perceptible ambiguous smile.
The metamorphosis of a high-minded idealistic dreamer into an
ordinary opportunist occurred frequently enough in the Russia
of the 1830's and 1840's, and Goncharov was right in treating
it with irony, i.e. in a tragi-comic vein. A tragi-comic element
persisted to some extent even in Goncharov himself, who projected quite a few of his own features into the young Aduyev.
In later years he acknowledged that while writing *A Common
Story* 'I had in view myself and other people like me'. Yet as an
artist he was content to show the blind-alley of such a fate, without proposing a way out. The truth is that Goncharov was here
concerned not with views but with people, whose artistic validity
can only be measured in terms of real and convincing characterization. When expressing his view at all, he showed it as an
inalienable part of some character, or as arising from a definite
situation, and that is about all we can demand from a novel.
It is to Goncharov's credit that he did it with skill and with a
subtly distilled sense of humour.

The eternal struggle between the old and the new in a Russian
setting is thus artistically impressive also on account of its
'ideological' inconclusiveness. One wishes, though, that Alexander were made more explicit during his last phase. There is
insufficient psychological motivation of the gap between the
disappointed romantic and the opportunist of the smug philistine
brand. Yet such a defect is easily compensated by the refreshing
concreteness of Goncharov's characters in general, even the
minor ones. He makes us see them both as people belonging to
definite social layers (masters, servants, officials, and so on) and
as individuals. In either case they are revealed to us largely by a
right choice of detail, and this again is strengthened by appropriate analysis. He sees them all as people taken straight
from life, and he makes us see them as such. Even the models
for some of his figures are known to us. The practical worldly-wise uncle Aduyev, for instance, is supposed to have been a
certain N. A. Solonitsyn, one of Goncharov's chiefs in the civil
service. And as for the young Alexander Aduyev, it stands to
reason that Goncharov put into him much of that romanticism
of which he wanted to rid himself.

There are also Goncharov's descriptions of the background,
both provincial and metropolitan. He is particularly good when

depicting the servants and members of the households of the country gentry he knew so well. And he always finds the right tone for them, with just that touch of humour which helps to enliven the conversational flow of his language. As a narrator Goncharov was anxious to preserve the simplicity and naturalness inherited from Pushkin. But at the same time he emulated Gogol's meticulous attention to detail as well. A. Druzhinin, one of the notable aesthetic critics produced by that generation, laid stress on the 'Flemish element' in Goncharov's writings. There is no denying that, owing to his dexterous use of *Klein-malerei*, he was at his best in genre-pictures, in the rendering of those scenes and interiors which he made all of a piece with the characters. Yet his realism, too, like that of Gogol, may camouflage a number of subjective elements. Both authors were prone to choose themes and details which were prompted by their own inclinations; by their conscious or unconscious inner needs.

This, incidentally, applies to Goncharov's handling of his principal theme, and goes a long way towards explaining the finale of this novel. To put it simply, he was all out for the birth of a progressive bourgeois-capitalist society in Russia, though not exactly of Aduyev's type and on Aduyev's lines. He sincerely wished to see the advent of active men who would enable his country to leave the cracking system of serfdom far behind and replace it by something truly worth while. Unconsciously, however, he remained so strongly rooted in the past, in the impressions and memories of his own childhood, that he could never rid himself of a secret nostalgia for the old feudal 'nests of gentle-folk' so full of cosy indolence and comfort. These two trends, contending in him throughout, were largely responsible for both the choice and the treatment of the subject-matter of his novels. The struggle between the old and the new, the antithetic (or shall we say 'dialectical') approach to the theme itself, and the irony it involved—they all seem to have sprung from Goncharov's own divided propensities. Hence the ambiguous conclusion of *A Common Story*: the apparent victory of the prosperous Alexander Aduyev was merely the beginning of defeat, the same defeat which saddened the approaching old age of his prosperous uncle.

Goncharov's next work, *Son Oblomova* (*Oblomov's Dream*, 1849), which he subsequently included in his great novel, was more in the nature of an escape from the hard and harsh realities of the time. Oblomovka, the estate of the dreaming hero, is really nothing but an intensified Arcadia of Alexander Aduyev's childhood as described in the first part of *A Common Story*. The description is however more minute this time, and its nostalgic flavour is reminiscent of Gogol's *Starosvetskie pomeshchiki* (*Old-World Landowners*): a realistic narrative on the surface, yet permeated by the romantic longing for the rural 'Paradise lost' which looks doubly attractive in the distance, especially when seen from the cold and bureaucratic Petersburg. The same applies to Oblomovka, or, for that matter, to Goncharov's family house in the distant Simbirsk:

> The sky there seems to come nearer to the earth, not in order to fling sharper arrows at it, but to hug it more warmly and lovingly; it hangs as low overhead as the trusty roof of the parental home, to preserve as it were the chosen place from all calamities. The sun there shines warmly and brightly for about six months in the year and then withdraws gradually, as though reluctantly turning back to have another look or two at the place it loves and to give it a warm, clear day amidst the autumn rains.
>
> The hills seem to be mere models of those terrible mountains far away that frighten one's imagination. They rise in gentle slopes, pleasant to slide down on one's back in play, or to sit on, dreamily watching the sunset.
>
> The river runs cheerfully, sporting and playing; now it spreads into a wide pond, now flows on in a rapid stream, and hardly moves along the pebbles, sending out to all sides lively brooks, the ripple of which makes one delightfully drowsy.
>
> The whole place, for ten or fifteen miles around, is a series of picturesque, bright and smiling landscapes. The sandy, sloping banks of the clear river, the small bushes that come down from the hill to the water, the curving ravine with a brook running through it, the birch copse—all seem to have been fitted together on purpose and drawn with a master's hand.

After many a glowing picture of this kind the author makes a comment to the effect that 'a heart worn out by troubles or wholly unfamiliar with them longs to hide in this secluded spot and live there happily, unnoticed by all. Everything there promises a calm, long life till the hair turns from grey to the palest yellow, and death comes unnoticed like sleep.' Such was the pleasant idyllic side of that existence which Goncharov tried to sacrifice to the spirit of a more enterprising and active age. But the old roots remained and had a power of their own which could not be ignored, whatever the demands of the *Zeitgeist*. The clash between the two trends was given a monumental expression in Goncharov's next novel, *Oblomov*.

III

Oblomov and Oblomovism

I

The general theme of Goncharov's *Oblomov* is similar to that of *A Common Story*, but here it is deepened into a tragedy of passivity and of that peculiar type of indolence which soon became connected with the name of Oblomov not only in Russia but also in other parts of the world. There were several Russian authors, including Gogol, who had tried to portray the lazy-bones in fiction, yet none of them was able to endow him with the roundness and reality typical of Goncharov's hero. For *Oblomov* is not only a picture of a passive, vegetative existence—it is also a great character study of arrested development; of that absolute inability (as well as unwillingness) to adapt oneself to life which instinctively shuns all effort and tends to keep the individual on the level of a child in a well-protected nursery. The impression it leaves is the stronger because of the humorous inflection peculiar to the author, mixed with an atmosphere of inevitable doom. Then there is Goncharov's usual skill at painting portraits in which one cannot but recognise a master's hand.

The novel was conceived not later than 1846 or 1847. In the summer of 1857, while at Marienbad, the author put most of the material together, and the work was at last allowed to appear in 1859. Those were the days when, after the fiasco of the Crimean campaign, there was a general hope for reforms, as well as for men strong and active enough to shoulder the tasks lying ahead.

Goncharov himself was all for reforms which would replace the system of serfdom by something better. Yet as an intellectual of the 1840's he realised only too well that the 'psychological' consequences of serfdom were often difficult to cope with even for some of the best of the gentry who were, after all, the guardians of what was fine and valuable in Russian culture. A class which, for centuries, had been thriving on the labour of serfs was bound to weaken its stamina by such a parasitic existence. Disposition towards inertia was even enhanced by certain aspects of the disconcertingly broad and monotonous Russian landscape. In his sketch *Na rodine* (*At Home*) Goncharov says that when, after his graduation, he came again to Simbirsk, 'the very exterior of my native town represented but a picture of sleep and stagnation'. The same sleep and stagnation persisted in thousands of other towns, villages and manors at a time when history was already clamouring for a change, in the name of a different future.

In Ilya Ilyich Oblomov, the hero of this novel, the author actually resumed the dilemma of Alexander Aduyev in *A Common Story*. To make the parallel all the stronger, Oblomov too had left his estate in search of a more active and useful life in Petersburg. He endured some two years in the civil service, but the forces to which he had surrendered were too much for him. What is more, they were the result of an extremely happy childhood on his ancestral estate of Oblomovka—the same kind of private paradise for the serf-owners as was the young Aduyev's Grachi. Snuggled somewhere in the backwoods, Oblomovka had an idyllic but indolent charm of its own which overwhelmed the boy and kept him in its grip for the rest of his life. He fell a prey to that charm the more easily because there was no need for him to exercise his initiative and will-power, or to make the slightest effort of any sort, since everything was done for him by the numerous servants who were always at his beck and call. In the end he found himself incapable of making a decision, even when confronted by the most obvious tasks of life. Sapped by the passivity and apathy he had inherited from generations of equally inert ancestors, he eventually became too lazy even to live—he only existed in a purely vegetative sense. This is why we find him, after a twelve years' stay in Petersburg, at the mercy of his day-dreams and of his old house-serf Zakhar—another typical product of Oblomovka, but on a lower moral and psychological level than his master.[1]

[1] An anticipation of both Oblomov and Zakhar can be found in Goncharov's story *Ivan Savich Podzhabrin*, which appeared in the January number of *The Contemporary* for 1848.

Not that Oblomov, now a man of thirty-two or three, was a bad specimen of humanity. On the contrary, the first impression he made on one was invariably in his favour. For 'neither weariness nor boredom could banish for a moment the softness which was the dominant and permanent expression not merely of his face but of his whole being. A serene, open, candid mind was reflected in his eyes, his smile, in every movement of his head and his hands. A cold and superficial observer would glance at Oblomov and say: "A good-hearted, simple fellow, I should think." A kinder and more thoughtful man would gaze into his face for some time and walk off in benevolent uncertainty.'

Wrapped in his soft oriental dressing-gown, Oblomov spent most of his time lying down or sitting around at home—as though mortally afraid of any contact with real life. The very start of the novel is marked by his awakening at eight in the morning and by his fright at the sudden recollection of a letter which has to be answered.

He was obviously suffering from an inward conflict, and his intellect had not yet come to his aid. The fact was that the evening before Oblomov had received a disagreeable letter from the bailiff of his estate. It was no joke! One had to think of taking some measures. In justice to Ilya Ilyich it must be said that, after receiving the bailiff's first unpleasant letter several years before, he had begun to think of various changes and improvements in the management of his estate. He proposed introducing fresh economic, administrative, and other measures. But the plan was not yet thoroughly thought out, and the bailiff's unpleasant letters came every year inciting him to action and disturbing his peace of mind. Oblomov knew it was necessary to do something decisive.

As soon as he woke, he made up his mind to get up and wash, and, after drinking tea, to think matters over, taking various things into consideration and writing them down, and altogether to go into the subject thoroughly. He lay for half an hour tormented by his decision; but afterwards he reflected that he would have time to think after breakfast, which he could have in bed as usual, especially since one can think as well by lying down. This was what he did. After his morning tea he sat up and very nearly got out of bed; looking at his slippers, he began lowering one foot down towards them, but at once drew it back again. It struck half-past nine.

The whole of the first part of the novel deals with the comedy of Oblomov's inability to get up. This process is interrupted by a few callers and by the periodic growlings of the lazy, clumsy and always cantankerous Zakhar. He seems to be at daggers drawn with Oblomov, whom he cheats, to whom he lies whenever he can, while yet remaining devoted to him with the admiration of a born servant for the man he regards as his master. The entire morning and afternoon are frittered away on Oblomov's repeatedly frustrated attempts to get up. More than a hundred odd pages deal with these attempts, yet they are written in so humorous a vein (especially the wrangles between Oblomov and Zakhar) that the reader cannot tear himself away. It is only at the very end of the first part that a different element steps in—in the person of Oblomov's old friend and schoolfellow Andrey Ivanovich Stolz.

2

Stolz is a counterpart of the energetic Peter Aduyev in *A Common Story*, while Oblomov is a kind of Alexander Aduyev manqué. The basic theme of Goncharov's first novel is here amplified by the addition of a number of characters, as well as by a minute rendering of Oblomov's background. Stolz again —'all bone, muscle and nerve'—is not a potential sceptic of his own activities (as Peter Aduyev became towards the end). On the contrary, he is shown to us as the best representative of that bourgeois-capitalist trend which Russia could no longer avoid. Nor is he entirely swamped by his acquisitive appetites. 'Just as nothing was excessive in his physique, so in his mental activities he aimed at a balance between the practical side of life and the claims of the spirit.' In this respect he was a definite moral improvement upon Peter Aduyev. Although half-German by birth, he was meant to be an all-round anticipation of the new active and 'positive' hero of whom Russia was so much in need. Yet taken as a whole, Stolz is the only major portrait in this work that may strike one as an abstraction rather than a convincing human being. The 'idea' certainly does stick out of the man, even too much so. Otherwise, it was as a contrast to Oblomov that Stolz was destined to play an important part in the novel as well as in his friend's life.

For one thing, he was aware not only of Oblomov's weakness and apathy but also of his good qualities. Knowing his intelligence and integrity, his 'honest and faithful heart' which was incapable of any false note, Stolz spared no efforts to rouse his friend and to make him live up to what was best in him. It was he who coined the word 'oblomovism' as an antithesis to his own active and constructive ideal of life. Oblomov himself—inseparable from his oriental dressing-gown and slippers—provided the best illustration of that nickname when complaining, during a talk with Stolz, about the strange inner paralysis he could neither shake off nor even understand:

> I have had no storms, no shocks of any sort, I have nothing on my conscience—it is clear as glass, no blow of any kind has shattered my ambitions, and God only knows why my life is such a waste! . . . Yes, I am like an old worn-out coat, and it isn't because of the climate or of work, but because for twelve years a fire has been shut up within me which could not find an outlet, it merely ravaged its prison and died down. Twelve years have passed, my dear Andrey: I do not want to wake up any more.

Stolz, however, was determined to rid his friend of 'oblomovism'. He did his utmost to drag him out of the mire, but all his efforts came to nothing. 'While I am with him he is ready to do anything, but as soon as I am out of sight, it's all over: he goes to sleep again. It's like trying to reform a drunkard'. Yet he went on trying. The severest test came after he had introduced his friend to Olga Ilyinskaya,[1] a fascinating girl of twenty, with whom Oblomov fell in love. She herself became attached to Oblomov, or to the phantom of Oblomov conjured up by her own wishful thinking. As she later confessed to Stolz, she had loved the Oblomov that could have been rather than the one she saw in the flesh. She did in fact all she could to make him wake up, and at first it almost seemed as though she would succeed. He proposed to her, was accepted, and felt radiantly happy, until the psychic and moral heritage of his Oblomovka began to assert itself. His aversion to all responsibility was increased, this time, by the practical aspects of marriage, especially by the financial difficulties caused by his own carelessness. He started putting off his visits to Olga, but while with her, he often made a thorough fool of himself. Failure came even sooner than either of them had thought.

[1] Olga Ilyinskaya was partly a portrait of Elizaveta Vasilyevna Tolstaya, to whom Goncharov became more attached than to a mere friend in 1855, after his return from Japan. But she preferred to marry one of her rich cousins.

'Why has all been wrecked?' she asked, suddenly raising her head. 'Who laid a curse on you, Ilya? What have you done? You are kind, intelligent, affectionate, noble . . . and . . . you are doomed! What has ruined you? There is no name for that evil.'

'Yes, there is', he whispered, almost inaudibly.

She looked at him questioningly, with her eyes full of tears.

'Oblomovism', he whispered; then he took her hand, wanted to kiss it and could not; he merely pressed it close to his lips and hot tears fell on his fingers. Without raising his face, he turned and walked out of the room.

But by that time he had already found a substitute for Oblomovka in the suburban house he had rented from the young and plump widow, Agafya Matveyavna Pshenitsyna (a wonderful portrait). Always busy, always displaying her white neck and rapidly moving elbows while at work in the kitchen, she was the quintessence of lower middle-class domesticity. No brains and all instinct, she radiated that docile maternal kindness and generosity in which sex played hardly any part at all. What made her the more attached to Oblomov was her realization that he was her social superior: a being of a higher order who had to be measured only by his own standards. Her maternal nature again was stirred by his very weaknesses to that devotion which she would have showered on her own two children had they fallen ill. Under the wing of Mme Pshenitsyna, Oblomov soon basked in the same selfless love he had found in Olga, but without Olga's demands upon him. Here he was sheltered from the worries or contacts with life; and could indulge in his 'oblomovism' to the exclusion of everything else. Eventually, Agafya, who had a child by him, became his wife—all according to the line of least resistance. It was an idyll with a hidden undertone of tragedy; the more so because having become Agafya's husband, he was doomed to absolute inertia. The unsettling kind of love he had cherished not so long ago for Olga was now out of the question once and for all.

He came closer to Agafya Matveyevna as one does to a fire which makes one warmer and warmer, but which cannot be loved. After dinner he readily remained in her room to smoke his pipe, watching her put away the silver and the dinner-service in the dresser, take out the cups, and pour out coffee; after washing and wiping one cup with special care she poured out his coffee first of all, handed it to him, and looked to see if he liked it. His eyes liked to dwell on her plump neck and rounded elbows when the door into her room was open, and if it had remained shut too long he gently pushed it open with his foot and joked with her or played with her children. But he did not miss her if the morning passed without seeing her; after dinner, instead of remaining with her, he often retired to have a couple of hours' sleep; but he knew that the moment he woke his tea would be ready for him. And the great thing was that everything went on peacefully: he had no lump at his heart, he never once wondered anxiously whether he would see his landlady or not, or worried as to what she would think, what he would say to her, how he would answer her question, how she would look at him—there was nothing of the kind. He had no yearnings, no sleepless nights, no sweet or bitter tears. He sat smoking and looked at her sewing, sometimes he said something and sometimes he said nothing, and all the time he felt at peace, not needing anything, not wanting to go anywhere, as though all he needed were here. Agafya Matveyevna incited him to nothing, made no demands upon him. And he had no ambitious impulses or desires, no longing to do something heroic, no agonizing regrets that time was passing and his powers were being wasted, that he had done nothing, either good or bad, that he was idly vegetating instead of living. It was as though some unseen hand had placed him as a precious plant in a spot where he was sheltered from the heat and the rain, and nurtured him tenderly.

In marrying Agafya, who submitted even to her intimate conjugal duties in the meek way a 'mare submits to her harness', Oblomov only acted according to his own immutable nature. What he really needed was not a wife but a mother. And as long as Agafya's maternal eye kept watch over him, he knew he was safe from any worries, big or small. He was back in his nursery—carefree once again and in his own way as happy as once he had been in his native Oblomovka. Even when, on rare occasions, he had suspicions of the human tragedy lurking behind that sloth of his, Agafya was always there to allay his fears and to set his mind and body at rest.

As was to be expected, after a few months of sadness, Olga was married to Stolz, who found in her not only a wife but an invaluable friend and companion as well. Oblomov, on the other hand, kept rolling downhill in his own pleasant and placid manner until, a few years later, death itself came to him in sleep, causing him as little trouble as possible. Yet the memory Oblomov left in all who had known him, Olga included, was that of a decent and lovable human being, sapped by forces which were beyond his control. Agafya could not get over her loss. Even the eternally grumbling Zakhar became only a shadow of his former self—a pathetic old beggar waiting for his own death. Life flourished, though, and glowed with new prospects and promises within the orbit of Stolz's realm. In fact it was Andrey Stolz who, after his last visit to Oblomov, summed up the meaning of his own activities. As though looking into the future of a changing Russia, he mentally addressed his friend:

It is no use telling you that your Oblomovka is no longer in the backwoods, that its turn has come and rays of sunshine have fallen upon it too! I won't tell you that, in another few years, there will be a station there, that your peasants will be working on the line and your corn will be carried by train to the river . . . And then schools, education . . . and beyond that . . . No, you will be alarmed at the dawn of the new happiness, it will hurt your eyes used to darkness. Good-bye, old Oblomovka, your day is passed.

3

So much for the social significance of this novel. To draw another parallel with *A Common Story*, Olga too, like Aduyev's wife, eventually feels apprehensive of her husband's bourgeois prosperity. She senses in it a danger, and does not mind saying so. Of even greater momentum in *Oblomov* is its psychological side, especially the gradual yet inevitable (as though decreed by fate) moral deterioration of its chief character. In the last portions of the novel in particular, the pathos of Oblomov's going to seed becomes so oppressive that the reader feels a genuine relief at his death.

There are no diatribes against serfdom in this book. As in Gogol's *Dead Souls*, we feel here only by implication the indictment of a system which was bound to ruin morally the very people who benefited economically from it. A prototype of Oblomov can be found in Tentetnikov—one of Gogol's characters in the preserved chapters of the second part of *Dead*

Souls.[1] The critic D. I. Pisarev actually went so far as to call *Oblomov* the 'highest generalisation of the pre-reforms squire-archic Russia reached until now in our literature'. And N. A. Dobrolyubov, whose essay *Chto takoe oblomovshchina* (*What is Oblomovism*, 1859) made the novel justly famous, not only pointed out the factors responsible for 'oblomovism', but referred to a whole gallery of those unadapted or unadaptable 'superfluous men' who penetrated into Russian literature via Pushkin's Onegin and reached their strongest expression in Oblomov. The 'superfluous man' actually became a pathetic institution of Russian letters, and remained so until 1917. For a while it even threatened to survive the bolshevist revolution.[2]

Oblomov and oblomovism soon became nicknames which went beyond any mere social contexts or allusions. Oblomov himself ceased to designate only one category of people, and became a realistic symbol for certain frailties which are to be found in most human beings. In his autobiographic sketch Goncharov stated several years later: 'What struck me above all was the image of Oblomov in myself and in others'. The literary historian D. N. Ovsyaniko-Kulikovsky proclaimed oblomovism to be a disease of the Russian national structure as a whole—a statement which is much too sweeping to be taken literally. More plausible is the fact that, whether intentionally or not, Goncharov created in his hero a kind of universal symbol.

In the same way as there are in each of us potential elements of Hamlet, Don Juan, Don Quixote and even of Faust, we only need to scratch our consciousness—and not very deeply either—in order to detect in it surprisingly large deposits of oblomovism. Far from being a prerogative of any 'national structure' as such, it lurks in every human being, waiting for its chance. After all, one of man's ineradicable features is his 'oblomovian' propensity towards the line of least resistance, indolence, passivity and those day-dreams which he cultivates in order to support his own sloth and comfort with a clear conscience. Goncharov has thus contributed to world literature a most appropriate 'arch-type' of that stagnation which so often stands in the way of man's growth and prevents him from facing the stern demands of life.[3] Viewed from this angle Oblomov represents the farthest

[1] Gogol's Kostanzhoglo (*ibid.*) is at the same time the prototype of Stolz.
[2] The principal character in K. Fedin's excellent novel *Goroda i gody* (*Cities and Years*, 1924) is a 'superfluous' revolutionary.
[3] The universality of Goncharov's Oblomov has been aptly stressed also by André Mazon in his book *Un Maître du roman russe* (1914).

possible contrast to Faust, for example, since the Faustean universe is one of action and of that ceaseless creative endeavour which aims even beyond happiness in the ordinary sense.

Oblomovism is actually a danger everyone is called upon to overcome. Its aspects may be as manifold as are its allurements, some of which Goncharov, too, was unable to escape. For like Oblomov he was tied by powerful irrational bonds to the idyll of his childhood, to his own 'Oblomovka' at Simbirsk. Do what he would, its voice became in the end even more powerful than the call of the new age which had been so eagerly taken up by Andrey Stolz. This irrational bond asserted itself fully in Goncharov's third and last novel. But before tackling it we must dwell on a few technical features of *Oblomov*.

4

Conceived in the 1840's, *Oblomov* matured slowly, and, since the date of its first appearance in 1859, it has won not only a national but an international fame. More colourful in style and richer in texture than *A Common Story*, *Oblomov* would yet hardly conform to the orthodox Western pattern of a novel. In this respect it is as thoroughly Russian as it could be. Its structure seems to be devoid of any plot. The stress is on the characters, on their mutual relations, and on the vital human element as such. There are no spectacular happenings in it, but just an unfolding of the chief hero's portrait to which everything else remains more or less accessory.

In his portraiture, however, Goncharov differs from the method of Dostoevsky or Tolstoy. He avoids those exceptional states of mind and spirit which abound in Dostoevsky's works. Nor does he concentrate on the essentials in order to imbue them, as Tolstoy does, with a stronger vitality than is to be found in life itself. Compared with these two, Goncharov may strike one at first as a tame or even pedestrian realist. He only believes in concrete physical details, for which he has an incredibly sharp eye, and which he arranges in such a way as to produce the effect of Flemish genre-pictures at their best. He can even build up, by means of them, a dramatic atmosphere when required, however undramatic he may be in his actual method. Such a cumulative handling of trifles brings about a rather slow tempo, though in Goncharov's case (as in the case of Marcel Proust) this is not a defect at all. Instead of becoming tiring, its slowness absorbs one by the very pertinence of the details. These we enjoy as we often enjoy the slowed down pace of a motion picture enabling us to see things which otherwise might well escape our attention.

Last but not least, there is Goncharov's humour, so different from that of Gogol for example. Gogol is not happy unless he exaggerates certain features at the expense of others to the point of grotesqueness. And this is precisely what Goncharov avoids. The forte of his humour is either in his tone, or else in a peculiar arrangement of obvious aspects and relations of life. There is not a tinge of deliberate caricature in the wrangles between Oblomov and Zakhar, yet we cannot help laughing at them as we do when reading Gogol. It was only after *Oblomov* that Goncharov made an attempt at deliberate parody. And this brings us to his next and last big novel, *The Ravine*.

IV

The Ravine

I

This novel took Goncharov some twenty years to write, during which process he repeatedly kept changing or even eliminating certain portions. Three of its fragments were published—between 1859 and 1861—in periodicals, but the whole work appeared for the first time in *Vestnik Evropy* (*The European Herald*) in 1869, that is, ten years after *Oblomov*. In some respects it was a logical continuation of the previous novel, since its principal hero, Boris Raisky, can be regarded as a man who has awakened, or is awakening (from Oblomov's 'sleep') in the more advanced conditions of the age, but does not yet know what to do either with the age or with himself. The canvas of *The Ravine* is rather broad, with plenty of incident, with a surprising variety of people, and as for its subject-matter, it bears the stamp of his two prolonged visits to Simbirsk—one in 1849 and the other in 1862. In one of his polemical articles Goncharov mentions the strongly antagonistic mixture of the old and the new he came across during the first of these two visits: 'Gardens, Volga, ravines in the environs, native air, reminiscences of childhood—all this invaded my mind and nearly prevented me from getting on with *Oblomov*, the first part of which was ready, while others were still in my imagination. But I brought back with me a new novel which I carried about in my mind and jotted down

37

on detached leaflets.' As the hero of this new work was originally meant to be an uprooted artistic dilettante, the author intended to call it simply *Khudozhnik* (The Artist), but for reasons of his own he later changed the title.

The struggle between the old and the new in an 'awakening' Russia groping towards her future through the layers of a traditional past is here if anything more dramatic than either in *A Common Story* or in *Oblomov*. The futile Hamlet-like Raisky (a typical 'superfluous man' of that period) has hardly enough guts to carry one through the whole of this long work. Goncharov himself acknowledged how difficult it was to shape a character endowed with so many talents and with so little backbone. Raisky wants to be a painter, a writer, a musician, eventually even a sculptor, without ever being able to decide which is his vocation. Devoid of a focus, he is doomed to remain a dilettante indulging in a continuous if rather sterile quest. This holds good even of his amorous adventures, in which his passion comes more from his imaginings than from his heart and blood.

Yet he has a flair for the new *Zeitgeist*. In fact, during his infatuation with the pretty aristocratic doll Sophia Belovodova at Petersburg, he does not mind rebuking her for her useless hothouse existence, typical of the privileged few. In an argument taking place in the portrait gallery of Belovodova's ancestors he looks at the busy street crowds below and flings at her: 'There, among them, there is life, whereas here is nothing but the cemetery'. Tired of the 'cemetery' of the past, as well as of his own futile life in Petersburg, Raisky suddenly decided—like Alexander Aduyev after his first Petersburg venture—to leave for his distant estate Malinovka. There, among his native haunts, he hoped to regain his peace of mind, without in the least suspecting the storms and the trials that can befall one even in such a quiet place.

Like Goncharov's own Simbirsk residence, Malinovka was situated on the outskirts of a Volga town. It also had the charm of Oblomov's ancestral seat—minus that inert and soporific atmosphere which had sapped the hapless Ilya Ilyich. Keenly alive to its beauty, Raisky could not but feel a criminal for having wasted so many years in Petersburg, 'scattering his emotions, chasing after forbidden fruits; while here nature herself kept a corner for him, full of sympathies and of happiness'. Such at least were his first impressions of that old corner ruled over by his great aunt Tatyana Berezhkova, commonly called 'granny', and adorned by his two pretty nieces, Marfinka and Vera.

38

In creating 'granny', Goncharov achieved a *tour de force*. She is an active 'positive' type, fully convincing and alive. Yet she is a member of the serf-owning caste—proud and bossy, at times even despotic; her manner leaves one in no doubt about that. Nevertheless her personality embraces all that was good and generous in old Russia. In her hostility to the new-fangled ways and ideas she clings to the social prejudices of her class. At the same time she is endowed with a broad tolerance, an understanding, and a sense of justice which earn her the love of all who come near her, Raisky included. Unfortunately she refuses to see that the world in which she lives has lost its stability.

Of the two nieces Marfinka is like 'granny': uninhibited, harmoniously balanced and made all of a piece. She would never swerve from her 'granny's' will or from the traditions in which she is rooted, since these are in her blood and in her innermost nature. Vera, however, is a different proposition. A literary descendant of Pushkin's Tatyana,[1] she has all the makings of the 'new woman'. She is elusive, somewhat mysterious and above all a proudly independent personality, incapable of any compromises where her affections and convictions are concerned. Small wonder that from the moment she appears the centre of gravity almost inevitably is transferred from Raisky to Vera. The actual dilemma of the novel, too, shifts to her; for in contrast to her younger sister Marfinka, Vera no longer feels quite at home in the old patriarchal world of 'granny', although subconsciously she is still in it and has retained its religious and moral values. However much she loves what is good at Malinovka, she yet finds it too narrow, and is anxious to take part in the broader aspirations of the age. It is the crux of this dilemma that eventually becomes her tragedy.

As it happens, the new age, or rather the new generation, here makes a spurious entry in the person of the 'nihilist' Mark Volokhov. A political exile under police supervision, Volokhov upsets the sleepy provincials by his lack of conventions in ideas, manners and morals. Endowed with a directness and even with a blunt honesty of his own, he yet strikes one as an uprooted cynic, a sponger, or even a cad who is very much in love with himself. In some respects Volokhov comes close to being a deliberate caricature of another 'nihilist'—Bazarov in Turgenev's *Ottsy i deti* (*Fathers and Children*), published some eight years earlier.

[1] The heroine of Pushkin's famous 'novel in verse', *Evgeny Onegin*.

Raisky, Vera, 'granny' and Volokhov thus become the central figures of this work. Raisky's love for Vera, harassed by a continuous process of jealousy, fills many of its pages. It also complicates the book technically by making Raisky try to write his own novel within the novel Goncharov writes about him. Then there is a galaxy of excellently drawn minor characters: town worthies, officials, landowners, house-serfs, all of whom help to enrich the pattern of the narrative. Yet taken as a whole the artistic level of *The Ravine* is lower than that of *Oblomov*. It is marred by psychological faults, and by a few inconsistencies as well.

2

One of these is the author's confusion of two different epochs. The style of life at Malinovka, for instance, is entirely that of the serfdom period, whereas Volokhov and Vera have the imprint of the emancipated era after 1861. Such overlapping can only be explained by Goncharov's two consecutive visits to his native town, in 1849 and 1862, the impressions of which are intermingled in the novel. The patriarchal life of the serfdom period, with 'granny' in the centre, is described as the author saw it in 1849. Judging by a few hints, the action takes place at the beginning of the 1850's—a period which was certainly premature for the appearance of a 'nihilist' such as Volokhov. Besides, Goncharov himself acknowledged that Volokhov was an afterthought. His first intention had been to portray a revolutionary liberal (of the best kind) married to Vera and followed by her into Siberian exile. After his visit to Simbirsk in 1862, however, the author changed his mind and presented his readers with a fashionable 'nihilist' instead; partly because during that visit he had met—so he says—several youngsters, including his own nephew, who resembled Volokhov. He may even have deliberately parodied a few features of his bugbear D. I. Pisarev, the chief critic on the staff of *Russkoe Slovo* (*The Russian Word*) whose reviews were not always generous to Goncharov's pen.

In the controversy that followed Goncharov tried to answer the outcry against Volokhov by asserting that he did not mean him to be a symbolic representative of the younger generation; but such statements *post factum* are rarely quite convincing. Be this as it may, the author here combined the serfdom period with the 'characters of an epoch which had not only discarded serfdom, but was busy introducing all sorts of other reforms too:

the *zemstvos* (provincial elective assemblies), the Western jury-system, a less rigorous censorship, and so on. After the Polish revolt of 1863-64 this tide received a setback, yet the liberal mood of the country could no longer be stemmed. The younger generation of that decade was particularly impatient. In contrast to their dreamy fathers of the 1840's, these realistic sons of theirs were fed on Büchner's *Kraft und Stoff*, as well as on the radical social and political ideas imported from the West. Unfortunately, in their hurry to advance them *à tout prix* these youths were often unable to digest them properly. What in Western Europe passed only for a theory, became—once it had been smuggled into Russia—a cult, a religion, leading to excesses or even downright distortions. The earnestness with which a new outlook was advocated by the 'nihilists' found its echo also in literature, beginning with Turgenev's Bazarov.

As a votary of science and action, Bazarov was ready to scrap the whole of old Russia, with her patriarchal obscurantism, in order to build up something better and really worth while. Such moods of the younger generation were corroborated by the leaders of radical thought—Chernyshevsky, Dobrolyubov, Pisarev, Herzen. In this fermenting process the University students in particular were addicted to all sorts of extremist views, even to those advocating violence. It did not take long before 'nihilism' found its practical expression in Karagozov's attempt on the Tsar's life in 1866. Three years later Russia was shocked by the gruesome Nechayev crime, subsequently recorded in Dostoevsky's novel *Besy* (*The Possessed*, 1871-72). Crime and terrorism in the name of ideas frightened many an intellectual and were responsible for a spate of anti-radical novels, in addition to Dostoevsky's well-nigh apocalyptic indictment. Leskov's *Nekuda* (*The Impasse*, 1864) and *Na nozhakh* (*At Daggers Drawn*, 1870) are cases in point. They aroused such indignation among the radicals that one of the critics proposed to 'expel' their author altogether from literature. Then there was Pisemsky, and among the lesser lights Krestovsky, Markevich, Klyushnikov, Avseyenko, and others.

In this tug-of-war there was one problem, however, which kept cropping up, directly or indirectly, all the time: the problem of Russia and Europe. The authors with a Western orientation definitely favoured the social-political and scientific ideas (not to mention the technical advance) coming from Europe. To others again, notably the Slavophils, all that came from the West was anathema. The moral, or rather the spiritual and

41

metaphysical impact of this problem was gradually worked out in Dostoevsky's novels with an uncanny insight into the deeper 'underground' currents of the process. The dilemma of Russia and Europe is conspicuous in Turgenev's novels as well, especially in *Dym* (*The Smoke*, 1867), in which both factions—the Slavophils and the 'Westerners'—received their share of ridicule.

As for Goncharov, he dealt with it in *The Ravine* where he made the 'nihilist' Volokhov threaten all those Russian traditions and values which were so splendidly embodied in 'granny'. In doing so Goncharov himself sided this time not with Volokhov's revolutionary slogans imported from the West, but with 'granny'. He beat a retreat in the direction of that very patriarchal system which, in his previous novels, he had tried to condemn. Furthermore, the moral indignation with which he attacked the 'nihilist' anticipated as it were Dostoevsky's onslaught some two or three years later. For Goncharov charged Mark Volokhov with nothing less than the crime of having 'lowered man to a mere physical organism and rejected all that was not animal-like in him. The mere process of life was proclaimed by him to be the goal of life. But while denying humanity in human beings who have a mind and are entitled to immortality, he yet preached a kind of new truth, a new frankness, and a new will to a better life, without being in the least aware that all this becomes superfluous if our existence is something casual and if human beings are degraded to a swarm of midgets in hot weather: mixing, bustling about, procreating, basking in the sun, and vanishing in this senseless process only in order to make room for another swarm of the same kind.'

3

The passage could have served as a slogan for Dostoevsky's *The Possessed*. It touches upon those very aspects which in Dostoevsky's opinion resulted from the Western ideas—either badly digested, or else carried by the Russian mind to extreme conclusions. Yet Goncharov abstained from probing this plane of the dilemma, even if he gave us the pointer to it. As though suspecting its pitfalls, he did not go any deeper, and confined himself to the sphere of *byt* (*mores*) during a critical transition period. He compared *The Ravine* to a small lake reflecting the 'state of fermentation, the fight between the old and the new' which was going on in those years. And since Volokhov here emerges as a standard bearer of the 'new forces' operating in

Russia, he cannot be lightly dismissed even as a parody. It is significant that originally Goncharov even wrote Volokhov's autobiography but did not include it in the novel. Anyway, he neither indulges in *Tiefenpsychologie* like Dostoevsky nor makes his 'nihilist' philosophize more than necessary. Volokhov's importance thus comes out mainly in his relations with Vera, and of course in his open antagonism to everything 'granny' stands for.

One will remember that in *A Common Story* Goncharov eulogised the new progressive forces of Russia, even though the epilogue is ironical as far as the two Aduyevs are concerned. In *Oblomov* the no less successful Stolz is an ethically improved edition of the same opportunism, this time working in good faith for a change that was much needed by Russia. Yet when in the 1860's the ultra-radical section of the intelligentsia began to push this need along a path which seemed to disregard all historical sense, and even ordinary common sense, many minds could not but ask the simple question: on what terms and at what cost was the 'awakening' of Russia (as distinct from Oblomov's lethargic 'sleep') to take place?

The Ravine was an answer, or at least a warning. Hence the antithesis that is so obvious in the novel: the solidly patriarchal world of 'granny' pitted against the hollow and destructive radicalism of Volokhov. Whereas most of the first half of the novel gives a series of 'Flemish' pictures of life at Raisky's manor, the second half is marked by Vera's love for Volokhov and by the intrusion of Volokhov's disintegrating element into the atmosphere of Malinovka. The focus thus shifts to Vera, whose unhappy love soon comes into the foreground as the climax of the novel.

What exactly could have made so independent and proud a woman as Vera fall in love with such a man as Volokhov is not quite clear. While answering at length his critics and detractors, Goncharov tried to explain Vera away as a victim of the struggle between the old and the new.

She did not want to live blindly, according to the precepts of her elders. Knowing how much of the old life had been outlived, she longed for a fresh, meaningful existence; she was anxious consciously to find and to accept the new *truth*, while retaining all that was solid, basic, best in the old life. She wanted not destruction but renovation. She did *not know*, however, where and how to seek . . . In her new friend she hoped to find support, enlightenment, truth, since she had sensed in him a kind of force, of fire and daring; but instead she found only a lie. Because of her inexperience and reserve she failed to recognise it at first; but once she had recognised it she proudly thought of changing that new lie to her old truth and making—through sheer force of love—the renegade accept her own faith, love and hopes.

But this is not explicit in the novel, although Vera herself says on one occasion that she had fallen in love with Volokhov not because he was different from other human beings, but mainly on account of his loneliness, his badly concealed inner devastation, and unhappiness behind which there was yet something potentially good and decent. 'I wanted that you, too, should live, become better, stand on a higher level than all the rest . . . I quarrelled with you because of your disorderly existence.' The analogy with Olga's attitude towards Oblomov thus becomes evident. It seems, though, as if Goncharov had been prompted in this case by a number of conflicting motifs simply in order to show his heroine's complex character. For one thing, Vera, with all her outward reserve, has really a passionate nature capable of being overwhelmed by her own impulses. In another article written about his novel Goncharov says that in depicting Vera he was 'carried away by the manifestations of passion in a pure and proud woman and by her struggle with it'. Still, neither statement is enough to explain why her love for Volokhov became a matter of life and death to her, or why she reacted so suddenly and so violently after her voluntary surrender to him. Indeed she refused to see him even after he had made an offer to marry her on her own terms rather than on his.

Vera's conscious independence, by virtue of which she had taken fate into her own hands, was evidently not strong enough to overcome her unconscious subjection to the old patriarchal world of 'granny'. So the onrush of repentance and nausea following upon her 'fall' brought her to the verge of utter collapse. She began to recover only through a gradual adjustment to the moral values as embodied in 'granny' who once, in her youth, had passed through a crisis similar to that of Vera and yet had got over it. After 'granny's' pathetic confession, the chief obstacle to Vera's moral recovery was removed. Her experience at the bottom of the ravine or 'precipice'[1] was to be

[1] The Russian word *obrýv* can be translated either as precipice or

left behind. What mattered to her from now on was no longer the Russia of Volokhov's 'new lie', but the old truth of 'granny's' Russia, the truth of Malinovka. And to make Vera's future recovery safe and certain, Goncharov sent her a wooer in the person of Tushin—another Stolz, but this time of pure Russian blood and dominated by 'granny's' outlook. As a blend of the old patriarchal tradition and the new enterprising spirit, Tushin also is an abstraction rather than a being of flesh and blood. On the other hand, he was meant to serve as a contrast to Volokhov, and especially to the ineffectual Raisky who, after his frustrated love for Vera, departed—this time to Italy—the same 'superfluous' dilettante as ever. But he had learned at least one thing: that even his patriarchal Malinovka was much less idyllic than it had seemed on the surface. 'How enormous and terrifying this simple life is in the nakedness of its truth', he exclaimed while leaving for abroad. And his exclamation would be a fitting motto for the novel as a whole.

4

Such is the gist of this bulky and somewhat rambling work, the last two parts of which are marred by Goncharov's didactic outbursts. Socially speaking, here is a man of the 1840's criticising the generation of the 1860's—sincerely, honestly, but with a mistaken idea of its aims and aspirations. Volokhov represents only the distorted aspects of what that decade was striving for. It was a clash between 'fathers' and 'children' who were no longer able to understand each other. Goncharov, being one of the 'fathers', was here obviously anxious to put forward his own attitude as against that of the young radicals of the 1860's. His very distortions may have sprung from his wish to make his point of view as clear as possible. 'In this work are transposed into images my own convictions, rules and impressions, and all this is taken from the good, healthy, and—I dare say—honest sources of life,' he wrote to Troitsky in July 1868, shortly before *The Ravine* was published. And years later he again stressed in his correspondence how closely this novel was connected with his own life: 'I put into it a part of myself, people who were near to me, my country, Volga, my native haunts, one can even say the whole of that life which had been mine and which I loved.'

ravine. The usual translation of the title of the novel is *The Precipice* which, in this case, has a trite 'symbolic' flavour. But the place where Vera and Volokhov used to meet was actually a ravine, with a summerhouse at the bottom of it. *The Ravine* is a preferable title.

It is not difficult to feel in Raisky quite a few of the author's own features, beginning with his boredom 'as wide, as barren as the steppe and inherent in life itself'. 'Granny', who had been turned into a symbol of old Russia, is supposed to embody certain traits of Goncharov's own mother. Also the prototypes of Vera and Marfinka are known.[1] Even the ex-naval officer Tregubov found a counterpart in the old-world gallant, Tit Nikonych Vatugin, whose worship of 'granny' was probably an echo of Tregubov's old secret love for Mme Goncharova.[2]

The Ravine thus became a kind of nostalgic *recherche du temps perdu*, as well as a judgment of the present from the standpoint of the preferable past. The real antagonists in the struggle between the two worlds are 'granny' and Volokhov, while Vera's flight from Volokhov back to 'granny' is the moral victory of the latter. But Goncharov must surely have known that such a wholesale triumph would not hold good for long. After all, Malinovka—even when purged of 'oblomovism'—was hardly a solution. So Tushin was called in as a possible *deus ex machina*: a man who combined the solid old roots with what looked good and promising in the trends of the new age.

That sounds like common sense. Still, it does not alter the fact that Goncharov, while growing old, felt more and more of a stranger not only with regard to the younger generation but to the quickly changing new world in general. He was so perplexed by it all that he even gave up his intention to write a novel about the decade which followed The Ravine. 'I gave up that plan', he confessed in one of his articles, 'because one's creative process demands a quiet observation of stabilized and settled forms of life, but this new life of ours is too new for me —it vibrates in its fermentation, assumes certain forms today, disintegrates tomorrow, and changes not from day to day but from hour to hour'.

The faults of The Ravine are obvious enough. Although a great success with the reading public, the novel was severely attacked by critics in the liberal and radical camps. Turgenev dismissed it simply as a 'novel written by an official for officials and their wives'—a statement which now sounds more summary than fair.[3] For with all its unevenness, The Ravine remains a

[1] They were Adelaide and Emilia Rudolf—sisters of his brother's wife.
[2] The account of 'granny's' old love for Vatugin, although written, like Volokhov's autobiography, was not included in the novel.
[3] Among the more recent instances D. S. Mirsky's one-sided verdict (in his *History of Russian Literature*) can be mentioned.

novel written by a great author (which need not be exactly the same as a great novel). It abounds in unforgettable pictures of provincial life, in fine characterization and in some of the best descriptions of the Volga landscapes that ever came from Goncharov's or any other pen. Its vitality has, moreover, been proved by its survival. Even in Soviet Russia new editions of *The Ravine* continue to entertain not thousands but millions of readers.

V

Expedition, Reminiscences and Polemics

I

Apart from the trilogy discussed, Goncharov has to his credit the important non-fictional *Fregat Pallada* (*Frigate Pallas*) which in bulk at least outstrips even his last and longest novel. Excellent though it be from a literary standpoint, this book is yet a paradox; for it gives a most unexciting (but far from boring) account of a most exciting experience. It describes nothing less than Goncharov's sea journey to the Far East and Japan on the Russian frigate *Pallas* at a time when Japan was still closed to European influences and largely also to European contacts in general. The Russian frigate, with some five hundred men aboard, was sent there on a trade mission—a journey which in those days was not only very long but very hazardous and full of unexpected trials and adventures. In spite of his love of comfort, Goncharov accepted all that,[1] and once the expedition was finished, he summed up his impressions of that two-years' long venture in a book which has since become a classic of its kind.

In his preface to the third edition (1870) of *Frigate Pallas* the author says that its genesis was due mainly to the letters he had been sending to various friends at home. The letters were completed by sketches, comments, meditations, and above all by extracts from the diaries he kept writing during the expedition. Most of the material was first published in periodicals; then it was collected, enlarged, and in 1858—about a year before

---

[1] It was actually Goncharov's friend, the poet Apollon Maikov, who was first invited to join the expedition as secretary to its leader Admiral Putyatin, but as he could not go, Goncharov went in his place.

47

Oblomov—appeared in two substantial volumes.[1] Later two supplementary chapters were added: *Cherez dvadtsat let* (*Twenty Years After*) in 1874, and *Po vostochnoy Sibiri* (*Through Eastern Siberia*) in 1891.

At first glance *Frigate Pallas* may well look somewhat puzzling on account of its motley character, suggestive of a pastiche; but this is precisely one of its charms. It is informal, chatty, humorous, and has the direct appeal of an extemporized work. It is also highly personal, in that it reflects throughout Goncharov's own outlook upon man, life, and the world. Some of the experiences recorded must have been extraordinary indeed, yet as if determined to resist anything 'romantic' Goncharov remained calm, and refused to be affected either by awe or admiration. In the sea storms in the Pacific he saw only disorder and ugliness, intensified of course by sea sickness. Even the most exotic landscapes failed to disturb his composure. He had a good eye, though, for obvious things, and the daily routine of the countries he visited rarely escaped his attention. He showed the same realistic attitude with regard to their climate, their customs and costumes, and especially to their food—an item to which Goncharov (like Gogol) was always rather partial. Even trade is not omitted in his discussions, and as for the civilized comforts resulting from trade, he often talks of them with the fervour of a *Kulturträger*. The book is full of autobiographic reminiscences. The very sobriety with which they are related seems to guarantee their authenticity.

2

The frigate on which Goncharov travelled left Kronstadt on October 7th, 1852. On reaching Great Britain (via Denmark) she stayed for a longish period at Portsmouth where considerable repairs had to be done. As this was Goncharov's first contact with Western Europe, he was not idle, and kept his eyes open, especially during his strolls in London. His impressions, whether good or bad, are summed up in one of the longest letters in the book. Being a typical denizen of Russia, where the slow 'agricultural' tempo prevailed, Goncharov could not but be struck by the pace of life he found in England. Although an admirer of Western achievements, he was yet taken aback by

[1] Three years earlier the portion dealing with the actual stay in Japan appeared in book form under the title *Russkie v Yaponii* (*The Russians in Japan*).

48

the mechanization of life he witnessed amidst all the 'colour-fulness of smoke, coal, steam and soot'. Here are some of his comments—whatever their worth—upon a pattern of existence which he saw, as a mere outsider and a passer-by, for the first time.

Not only the public activities but the whole of English life is arranged so as to function like a practical machine. There is no evidence that public and private virtues spring here freely from a radiant human source, the spontaneous charm of which should be felt and enjoyed by the community. On the contrary, here everything seems to exist because it is required for the sake of some aim or some special reason. It seems that honesty, justice, compassion, are obtained like coal; so that in statistics one can mention—together with the accounts about steel production and textiles—the fact that, because of such and such a law, such and such a region has achieved so much jurisdiction; that such and such mass measures have decreased the noise, softened the manners, and so on. Measures of this kind are applied wherever necessary, and they keep turning round like wheels; hence their lack of warmth and charm. If you look at people's faces, at their actions and movements, you see there a practical awareness of good and evil as a duty, and not as life itself which should be enjoyable and fascinating. This is why the machine of public activities moves infallibly—a state of affairs which requires a great deal of honour and justice enforced by the severity of the law. The community prospers; its freedom and private property are sacrosanct. But for this very reason there exist cracks which are too narrow for the law to be squeezed in and where the control of public opinion is impotent. It is here that people find ways and means of doing things on their own; the public machine gets out of gear, and its wheels spin round in the air.

After a number of similar observations the author suddenly switches to a genre-picture of his homeland and rounds it up with the remark that no matter where he may go or be, his own native 'Oblomovka' invariably clings to him. In a way it clung to him during the whole of his journey—right to the shores of Japan, which the frigate touched at Nagasaki after some eleven months at sea. Before that she had stopped at Madeira, Cape Town, Java, Singapore, Hong Kong, and several other places, each more exotic than the last. From Nagasaki she made her way to Shanghai, Manila, Korea, but after a second brief call at Japan she had to look for safety in Siberian waters: a wise precaution, since the Crimean war was already on the way.

During all those months Goncharov preserved his usual quiet and composure, as well as his aversion to anything savouring of the 'grandiose'. His central experience consisted of his impressions of the conservative old Japan which the Russians reached in the middle of September 1853. Most of this section—the country, the officials and their manners, all sorts of encounters, banquets and not particularly successful trade negotiations—are described with delightfully understated humour. He is less humorous, though, when dealing with Hong Kong and Shanghai. His remarks about the opium traffic imposed upon China by a civilized Christian nation are far from complimentary.

As the expedition seemed to be dragging on indefinitely, Goncharov began to feel bored. His taste for the comforts he had enjoyed in the Russian capital now turned into a definite longing for home. 'Has there ever been a Ulysses who, sailing back from afar, did not look with his eyes for Ithaca?' His own Ithaca was of course Petersburg, whither he now started his return journey (amidst new hardships) through the whole of Siberia in August 1854. In February of the next year he reached his goal and resumed the routine of his double life: an official by profession and a writer by vocation.

3

Frigate Pallas appeared in print when *Oblomov* was already completed or at least nearing its completion, and while *The Ravine* was still in its initial stages. Although not a work of fiction, it enhanced the reputation of Goncharov whose next novel had been eagerly awaited since the success of *A Common Story*. *Frigate Pallas* was however far from being the only work in which he relied solely on facts, observation and reminiscences. During the last twenty years of his life, when his creative urge, as well as his understanding of the *Zeitgeist*, began to flag, he relied more on what he had seen earlier than on what he was seeing around him at the time. Yet after the unfavourable reception of *The Ravine* by the young radicals, Goncharov wrote his autobiographic apology, *Luchshe pozdno chem nikogda* (*Better Late than Never*, 1870, first printed in 1879), in a polemical mood, mainly in order to prove to his critics, or rather to the entire younger generation, that he was not as inaccessible to the spirit of the age as they would have it. He argued, more-over, that not only did his three novels, and especially the last one, reflect the three consecutive decades between 1840 and 1870, but that *The Ravine* in particular was better than anything he had written before. In his polemical ardour he actually turned this article into a kind of literary manifesto. While dealing with views on art and letters, he drew a distinction between the 'artistic truth' and the 'truth of nature' to the effect that a thing could be more *real* for the very reason that it was not real-istic in a purely photographic sense. In the course of his attack on naturalism, as well as on all tendentious and utilitarian 'art without art' (as propagated by many radicals) he paid a warm tribute to Dickens.

There are four other writings worth mentioning, which he completed in the eighteen-seventies: *Universitetskie vospo-minaniya* (*My University Reminiscences*, written probably in the early 1870's), *Million terzaniy* (*A Million Torments*, 1872), *Zametki o lichnosti Belinskogo* (*Notes about Belinsky's Person-ality*, 1874) and *Literaturny vecher* (*A Literary Evening*, 1877).

The first of these gives a sympathetic picture of what Moscow University was like in the early eighteen-thirties when there was (for a while) relative freedom of lectures and plenty of enthusiasm among the students. He draws vivid portraits of various pro-fessors who had left their mark on that period: Nadezhdin, Shevyrëv, Pogodin, and others. Among his first-year colleagues was the poet Lermontov—a youth with a 'swarthy, bloated face showing as it were oriental extraction, and with black, expressive eyes. He seemed to me apathetic, spoke little, and always sat in a lazy position, reclining on his elbow'. Goncharov never met him personally. His brightest memory was the visit Pushkin, then at the height of fame, paid to the University where he had an open argument with Professor Kachenovsky about the authenticity of the old-Russian masterpiece, *Slovo o polku Igoreve* (*The Lay about Igor's Campaign*).

In *A Million Torments* Goncharov made an excursion into criticism. This is a brilliant analysis of Griboyedov's classical comedy, *Gore ot uma* (*The Misfortune of Being Clever*, 1823), with a stress on its two main characters: Chatsky and Sophie. Chatsky is defended as a fully convincing and *necessary* rebel against a period he has outlived. In Sophie, however, Goncharov points out the subtle contradiction between her 'social' vices on the one hand, and on the other the hidden inclinations of her better personal self. Needless to say, the author is on the side

51

of Chatsky's outbursts and invectives. All the other characters undergo a similar scrutiny, the value of which has not been impaired by the passage of time. No one interested in Griboyedov's work can afford to ignore this essay.

Compared with it, *Notes on Belinsky's Personality* looks more casual. This was due, no doubt, to the fact that it was meant to be simply 'notes' for the benefit of the literary historian A. N. Pypin who was writing a biography of the great critic at the time. Most of Goncharov's remarks about Belinsky are apt, and some of them shrewd—for example that Belinsky was carried away by literary works in the same manner as Don Juan used to get infatuated with women, and often with similar results.

The reader is faced by something more involved (both in shape and character) in *A Literary Evening*, partly because this lengthy hybrid falls not between two but three stools: social 'reportage', fiction, and polemics. Its frame is that of a narrative, or rather an account of a gathering in an aristocratic house. The large gathering takes place in connection with the reading of a novel, the brief rendering of which forms the core of the story. Having drawn a number of quick portraits, Goncharov gives a somewhat ironical summary of Count P. A. Valuyev's now forgotten high-life novel, *Lorin*. The discussion after the reading assumes a polemical character. In it Goncharov contrives to air (with his tongue in his cheek) his own views about art, literature, Russia and many things besides. In the end it transpires that the provocative *enfant terrible* of the discussion was a famous actor in disguise who had deliberately fooled the entire company by pretending to be *un ours mal léché* and a kind of literary Volokhov.

4

There still remain the few writings done by Goncharov during the last decade of his life. Of these *Na rodine* (*At Home*, 1887) reads like a piece of autobiography, and an interesting one at that. It is a long fragment, although the span of life described in it is one year only—the one he spent in Simbirsk (in 1834-35) when making his debut in the civil service. It is all done with plenty of good humour, however much he may have resented the apathy and stagnation of his native town. He actually makes the remark that his idea of 'oblomovism' goes back to those impressions of Simbirsk and of some of its otherwise amiable citizens, beginning with Tregubov (whom he here calls Yakubov). His portraits of the easy-going philandering Governor, the local landowners, officials and bribetakers are most amusing; so is his picture of the general provincial atmosphere, seasoned with a number of anecdotes. The narrative ends with the arrival of the author, among the colourful suite of the suspended Governor, in Petersburg.

Portraits of an anecdotal kind, drawn entirely from reminiscences, can be found in one of Goncharov's last works, *Slugi starogo vremeni* (*Old-Time Servants*, 1888). Its heroes are four valets he had employed at different times. Like Oblomov's Zakhar, they were all somewhat odd and unusual; but their oddities are described with the author's tolerant sense of humour.

Of Goncharov's posthumous writings the comic sketch *Maï mesyats v Peterburge* (*The Month of May in Petersburg*) is full of good observation, but his story *Prevratnost' sud'by* (*The Inconstancy of Fate*) is frankly mediocre. Both appeared in the periodical *Niva* (*The Cornfield*) in 1892 and 1893 respectively. The already mentioned *Neobyknovennaya istorya* (*The Uncommon Story*), written in the second half of the eighteen-seventies and first published in 1924, is a document the interest of which is pathological rather than literary. Goncharov's reviews and occasional *feuilletons* printed in various periodicals are beyond the scope of this study;[1] so are the fragmentary stories and sketches unearthed by Soviet scholars since the revolution.

All this can serve as a proof that Goncharov's monumental work came to an end with *The Ravine*. His writings after 1869 added hardly anything to what had been said in his novels. These novels are, however, significant enough to secure for their author a permanent place in the republic of letters.

VI

Goncharov's Realism

I

The first thing which is likely to strike a reader of Goncharov's work is the absence of anything 'striking'. Having inherited Pushkin's naturalness and simplicity, he was, as it were, the opposite pole to Dostoevsky. Dostoevsky, whose realism was

---

[1] *Goncharov*, edited by A. P. Rybasov (Leningrad, 1938), contains a good collection of his literary-critical articles, notes and letters.

more visionary than visual, was all the time on the look-out for the exceptional or the abnormal. He revelled in that fermentation of inner life where all contrasts meet in a chaotic flux and the greatest antinomies exist side by side. Goncharov, on the other hand, stuck to his own realism of the obvious which he yet turned into something significant. Dostoevsky's 'second sight' was stronger than that of his eyes. With Goncharov it was the eyes that mattered first of all, and they certainly saw at once every trifle worth seeing. Take this simple and in its way so concrete description of the first meeting between Agafya Matveyevna and Oblomov, who has just taken rooms in Agafya's house.

Suddenly the door behind him creaked slightly, and the woman whom he had seen with a bare neck and elbows came into the room. She was about thirty; her skin was very fair and her face so plump that it seemed as though the colour could not find its way to her cheeks. In the place of eyebrows she had two slightly raised shiny patches with scanty, fair hair growing on them. Her greyish eyes were as simple and candid as the whole expression of her face; her hands were white but coarse, with knotted blue veins standing out. Her dress clung to her figure: one could see she used no artifice, not even that of wearing an extra petticoat to increase the size of her hips and make the waist look smaller. And so, even when she was fully clothed but had no shawl on, she could without detriment to her modesty have provided a sculptor with the model of a fine, well-developed bosom. Her dress looked old and worn in comparison with her smart shawl and best bonnet. She came in timidly and stopped, looking shyly at Oblomov.

This portrait, taken as it were from a 'Flemish' interior, is only one of the many illustrations of Goncharov's love for what is obvious, normal and homely. Nor would he ever separate his characters from their background and their external accessories, since he himself was always so fond of stabilized and settled patterns of existence in general. Such was the pattern of Russian life he had known before the reforms of 1861, and he clung to it in his novels in spite of his dislike of serfdom and of the evils arising from it. The fact is that as author and creative artist he felt perfectly at home in that pattern so long as it had remained stable. When sudden and drastic changes began to occur he felt less sure, and was likely to lose his orientation.

His interest in the plot as such was rather slight. He preferred to handle the material taken straight from actualities around him and to transform by his imagination the truth of life into the truth of art without severing the link between the two. This is why human relations, as he saw and understood them, always play the central part in his works, no matter what the social or ethical import of his novels may otherwise be. His stress is on character, especially on the main character, whom he usually introduces to the reader even before any action takes place. In doing this, Goncharov always knows his limits, and therefore prefers to remain in his own region of *terre-à-terre*, even at the risk of over-indulging in the 'Flemish' element.

In some respects it was his sense of proportion that prevented him from aiming either at undue heights or depths. And in his case the sense of proportion implied just enough amused irony to make his 'pedestrian' attitude towards life not only bearable but intensely interesting. His intelligent scepticism never seemed to have disturbed even the traditional tenets of his Christian faith. As in the case of Montaigne, it became an Epicurean cushion on which to rest, rather than a heavy stone weighing him down. His moderation may look to a superficial observer somewhat philistine; yet there was wisdom (of a kind) in it. For one thing, it saved him not only from the bleak despair of a Flaubert or Gogol, but also from the jeering invectives of a Saltykov-Shchedrin. In the case of Volokhov only, in *The Ravine*, Goncharov exchanged his tolerant irony and humour for more direct attacks; but even here he beat a retreat as soon as he realised that he had committed an unnecessary *faux pas*.

Like all the best Russian realists of that period, Goncharov wrote mainly about the gentry. His novels are epics of the Russian manor between 1840 and 1860 or thereabouts, even when the action—in *Oblomov*, for instance—takes place only in Petersburg. It was against this and partly against the bureaucratic background (both of which he knew well) that he shaped his characters—a process during which his memory, observation and imagination went hand-in-hand with his analytical gift. All this had to grow and to mature in him for years before it crystallized in his novels where his objective and subjective methods met, as it were, on equal terms.

'What has not grown within me, what I have not personally seen, observed, experienced, is inaccessible to my pen', he says in *Better Late than Never*. 'I have (or had) my own field,

my own ground, in the same way as I have my own native country, native air, my friends and enemies, my own world of observations, impressions and memories—so I wrote only about
what I had personally experienced, thought, loved, seen at close
quarters and grown familiar with'... 'And now apropos of
objectivity', he continues (through his mouthpiece) in *A Literary
Evening*, 'our new authors want to stretch it too far. It is true
that an artist should not intrude with his own person into the
picture. On the other hand, his spirit, imagination, thought,
feeling, are bound to permeate his work—so that it should be
a body created by the living spirit and not the accurate description of a corpse, or the product of some impersonal wizard.
The living bond between the artist and his work should be felt
by the spectator and the reader.'

2

Having thus drawn the line between what he calls 'protocolism'
and creative realism, Goncharov felt on safer ground. He also
took good care to depict many of his characters in such a way
as to turn them into both individuals and representatives, or
even realistic symbols, of entire social groups. Of Nadinka
(in *A Common Story*) who certainly is a definite person in her
own right, he says: 'I depict in her not Nadinka, but the Russian
girl belonging to a certain *milieu*. I myself happened to know not
one but many Nadinkas.' And what about Oblomov, Agafya,
Raisky, and 'granny'? As long as he takes them from the strata
he knows well, they are perfectly alive, convincing, and often
superb. He is paler and weaker, though, when tackling a less
familiar background—that of Belovodova, for instance, or of
Stolz and Tushin. Also the portraits of house-serfs in his novels
are excellent, especially that of Zakhar in *Oblomov*. Yet actual
peasants are practically absent from his narratives, since he knew
them badly or not at all.

Relying on his artistic instinct, he thus rarely went wrong.
This same instinct was also responsible for the balance between
the conscious and the unconscious elements in his works. Here
is what he has to say about it in *Better Late than Never*:

While drawing, I rarely know at that very moment what
my image, portrait, character means; I only see it alive before
me and watch in how far my design is true. I see it interlaced
in action with others—consequently I see scenes and at once

56

draw those others, sometimes far in advance of the plan of my novel, without guessing as yet how all the parts scattered in my mind will eventually blend into one whole . . . I myself get bored with my writing, until there is a sudden flash of light which shows me the path I should walk on. I always have a principal image which leads me on—and while marching to my goal I seize what comes along, that is, all that is relevant to it.

In his art, at any rate, he tried to reconcile the conscious and the unconscious elements, however much these may have been at cross-purposes in his life. We know that the discrepancy between the two led to a number of 'complexes' and phobias from which he suffered in his old age—and not only in his old age. It is no secret that he resented the bureaucratic duties which interfered with his literary inclinations. His descriptions of bureaucracy and bureaucrats bear the ironic tone of a man who is not exactly over-awed by admiration. Nor would Goncharov have retired at the age of fifty-six had he found the civil service more to his taste. So much for the treatment of officials and officialdom in his works.

Another discrepancy, which has a bearing upon his novels, came out in his attitude towards the progressive and liberal trends of the time. Consciously he not only sympathized with them, but in his first two novels he did his best to endorse what he regarded as progress. In the deeper layers of his unconscious, however, he yet remained tied down to his own 'native Oblomovka' which eventually, in The Ravine, began to play havoc with his liberal sympathies. Vacillations and contradictions of this kind make a study of his realism as well as of his personality all the more inviting, though not invariably easy.

Like the majority of novelists of that period, Goncharov allotted much space to love in his writings. In matters of sex he never went beyond the boundaries of Victorian prudishness; yet his attachment to Elizaveta Vasilyevna Tolstaya, in 1855, was itself enough to make him acquainted with passion and frustrated love, both of which he analyzed very well indeed.

His portraits of women, too, are among the most successful in Russian fiction. Nadinka in A Common Story, Olga and the widow Agafya Pshenitsyna in Oblomov, 'granny' and her two nieces in The Ravine, are unforgettable. And what could be more convincing than the rapprochement between Oblomov and Agafya—the simple woman whose devotion made it possible for her tenant and subsequent husband to continue his vegetative existence not only with a clear conscience, but even with all the semblance of self-respect.

<h2 style="text-align:center">3</h2>

As for the architectural side of Goncharov's novels, *A Common Story* shows practically no flaws in its almost too 'logical' structure. We should not forget, though, that this is his shortest novel—almost a *nouvelle*, and even this work Belinsky found crammed with 'enough material for ten novels'. The canvas of *Oblomov* and especially of *The Ravine* is much wider, so their structure is bound to be less compact. Yet in spite of their rambling character, these two novels are equally crowded with content. And however pathetic their *dénouement*, they are both permeated with that peculiar sense of humour which, incidentally, Goncharov regarded as a necessary ingredient (together with imagination) of any creative art.

In one of his essays Dmitry Merezhkovsky calls Goncharov the greatest Russian humourist after Griboyedov and Gogol—a statement which surely needs some explaining. Goncharov created a number of comic figures and situations, but his comicality differs from Griboyedov's caustic wit, from the grotesque exaggerations and the 'laughter through tears' of Gogol, as well as from the Swiftean satire of Saltykov-Shchedrin. Like the English humour, that of Goncharov too is disciplined by a strong sense of proportion on the one hand, and by a mildly ironical view of life on the other. Often it does not depend on what he says but on how he says it, that is, on the tone or the inflection he uses.

One of the deeper roots of Goncharov's humour may have been embedded in the split between his vocation and his profession, between his repressed romantic inclinations and his sober scepticism. The divergence between the two could always be vented, temporarily at least, through his irony, and sublimated through his humour which was only another name for his sense of proportion. When, in the second half of *The Ravine*, this sense had suddenly weakened, the *raisonneur* or even the preacher emerged, to the detriment of the artist. The author was driven into a tight corner from which he could no longer come to terms with the age in which he lived. So he naturally turned to the past. Feeling that there was nothing more he was able to say to the younger generation, which was impatiently waiting for a vivifying word, he now lost also that 'general image' which had helped him create his trilogy. All he wrote from then on was on a small scale, fragmentary, and feeding on *le temps perdu*. And the present? It had to be endured rather than enjoyed—endured amidst the boredom of a more and more isolated personal existence.

4

It is here above all that a parallel between Goncharov and Gogol can be drawn, since the creative genius of both had lost its impetus while they were still comparatively young. Gogol's influence upon Goncharov has already been mentioned. Goncharov himself said at the time: 'The Pushkin-Gogol school still continues, and we authors are only working out the material bequeathed to us by them.' But quite apart from that, it is worth mentioning that both Gogol and Goncharov reached in their works an impasse out of which there seemed to be no outlet, except the intense though questionable bourgeois activism of Kostanzhoglo (in the unfinished second part of *Dead Souls*) in the case of Gogol, and of Stolz and Tushin in the case of Goncharov.

Both of them were thus landed in that kind of ethical philistinism (to use a phrase coined by Ivanov-Razumnik) which opens hardly any other perspective except the prosperity of successful, if decent and virtuous, 'kulaks'. Gogol's case was, of course, the more tragic of the two. His personality may often strike one as being more confused than complex; yet it contained all the ingredients of that *Angst* which reached its climax in Dostoevsky and gradually began to spread also in the West like a spiritual epidemic.

Goncharov, on the other hand, was spared at least the excesses of such inner travail. As novelist he was too much of an artist, and as man he was endowed with too strong a common sense (even 'pedestrian' common sense) to indulge in excesses of any kind. Yet he, too, like Gogol before him, eventually adopted an attitude which can best be defined as an apology of the past. And he did this at the very moment when Russia herself was anxious to leave much of that past behind in the name of a better future. Accustomed to a slow and organic pace of life, Goncharov found the various changes too sudden and was much too apprehensive of the hectic revolutionary moods typical of the 1860's. Estranged from the present, he naturally turned his nostalgic look towards the past. Diffident of the age, as well as of his contemporaries, he withdrew into his own shell, from which he was released only by death.

VII

Conclusion

There is a tendency to regard Goncharov—like Swift, or Griboyedov—as a *homo unius libri*, which is a mistake. It is true that *Oblomov* represents the height of his creative power. This does not imply, however, that his two other novels are unimportant. They not only have merits of their own, but (as the author himself had pointed out) they form, together with *Oblomov*, a kind of trilogy showing the social, mental and moral climate of Russia during one of the most interesting transition periods in her history. Yet however superb his portraits and their setting, we cannot help feeling in him a certain incongruity between his strong sense of reality (or realities) on the one hand, and his sense of values on the other. Had the latter been adequate to the deeper social needs of the time in which he lived, he might have avoided at least some of the misunderstandings he suffered from in his old age.

Fortunately, it is not this aspect of his work that matters to us at present, however interesting it may be if seen in its historical perspective. What is important to us here and now is Goncharov's art, i.e. his interpretation of life in terms of fiction. It was in his fine description of human characters and of human relations that he transcended his own epoch. The things he said about them, as well as the manner in which he said them, have not lost their significance, however remote their setting may be from us both in space and time. In short, Goncharov the creative novelist is still alive. While remaining one of the leading figures in Russian literature, he also occupies a niche of his own in the literature of the world. What is best in his work is strong and vital enough to justify such a claim.

BIOGRAPHICAL NOTE

1812   Born in Simbirsk on the 6th (18th, new style) June.

1822   Went to Moscow School of Commerce.

1831-34 Studied at the University of Moscow.

1834-35 Civil servant at Simbirsk.

1835   Arrived in Petersburg, where he took up a post in the Ministry of Finance.

1839   His first story, *A Lucky Error*, appeared in Maikov's private miscellany, *The Moon Nights*.

1846   Goncharov met Belinsky.

1847   *A Common Story.*

1848   *Ivan Savich Podzhabrin.*

1849   *Oblomov's Dream.*

1852   Left in October on the frigate *Pallas* for Japan as secretary of the Russian commercial mission.

1855   Returned home in February (via Siberia).

1855   *The Russians in Japan.*

1858   *Frigate Pallas.*

1859   *Oblomov.*

1856-60 Goncharov worked in the department of censorship.

1862   Editor of *The Northern Mail.*

1863-67 Member of the Board of the Press.

1867   Retired.

1869   *The Ravine.*

1870   *Better Late Than Never*, and also *My University Reminiscences.*

1872   *A Million Torments.*

1874   *Notes about Belinsky's Personality.*

1875-76 *An Uncommon Story* (published 1924).

1877   *A Literary Evening.*

1887   *At Home.*

1888   *Old-Time Servants.*

1891   Goncharov died on the 15th (28th, new style) September.

BIBLIOGRAPHY

The various Russian editions of Goncharov's collected works (*Polnoe sobranie sochineniy*) appeared at Petersburg in 1884-87, 1899, 1909-12, 1916.

Fregat Pallada, Paris, 1935.
Izbrannye sochineniya (Selected works, consisting of his three novels), Moscow, 1948.
Putevye pis'ma Goncharova (*Goncharov's Travel Letters*), edited by B. M. Engelhardt, Moscow, 1932.
Literaturno-kriticheskie statyi i pis'ma (*Literary-Critical Articles and Letters*), edited by A. P. Rybasov, Leningrad, 1938.

English Translations

A Common Story, translated by Constance Garnett, Heinemann, 1890 and 1917.
Oblomov, translated by C. J. Hogarth, Allen and Unwin, 1915; translated by Natalie Duddington, Allen and Unwin, 1929; the same translation in 'Everyman's Library', 1932, Dent (London) and Dutton (New York).
The Precipice (*The Ravine*), Hodder and Stoughton, 1915. The name of the translator is not given, but the translation itself is much abridged and misleading.

French Translations

Simple Histoire, translated by E. Halperine, 1887.
Marc le Nihiliste, an abridged and unreliable adaptation of *The Ravine* by E. Gothi, 1886.
Oblomoff, translated by Hélène Izvolsky, 1926.

Italian Translation

Oblomov, translated by Professor E. Lo Gatto, Torino, 1929.

Some Biographical and Critical Studies
In Russian:
    I. A. Goncharov, by V. I. Pokrovsky, 1907.
    Goncharov, by E. A. Lyatsky, Stockholm, 1920.
    Roman i zhizn (*Romance and Life*), by E. A. Lyatsky, Prague, 1925.
    Goncharov, by V. E. Maksimov, 1925.
    I. A. Goncharov, by A. G. Tseitlin, 1950.

In other languages:
    E. Zabel, *Russische Litteraturbilder*, 1899.
    A. A. Mazon, *Un Maître du roman russe, I. A. Gontcharov*, 1914
    E. Lo Gatto, *L'Oblomov e l'oblomovismo* (from *Saggi sulla cultura russa*) 1923.
    W. Rehm, *Gontscharov und die Langeweile* (in his book *Experimentum medietatis*) 1947.

DATE DUE